THE BUTTERSCOTCH
LOVER'S COOKBOOK
& MAIL-ORDER TREATS SOURCE GUIDE

BY DIANA DALSASS

Library of Congress Preassigned Control Number: 2001129034

ISBN: 0-9709677-7-2

Printed in China by Everbest Printing Co.
through Four Colour Imports, Ltd.,
Louisville, Kentucky

Book Design: Julia Nourok
Cover Design: Studio 22.02
Cover Photograph: Steven Mark Needham
Interior Photographs: Zeva Oelbaum (page 39)
André Baranowski (page 47)
Mark Ferri (page 77)
Steven Mark Needham (all other photographs)

Library of Congress Cataloging-in-Publication Data

Dalsass, Diana.
       The butterscotch lover's cookbook : and mail-order treats
   source guide / Diana Dalsass.
          p. cm.
       Includes index.
       ISBN 0-9709677-7-2 (paper)
       1. Desserts. 2. Cookery (Butterscotch) I. Title.

TX773.D24 2001
641.8'6—dc21   2001035515

To Lori Gosset, who was instrumental in persuading me that the butterscotch lovers of the world have been sorely neglected.

Although I have written five previous cookbooks, this is the first one I have self-published, and I wish to acknowledge several people who have guided me through this process, including: My sister, Julia Nourok, who spent countless hours on the design of the book; Mark Gorenstein, who so creatively furnished me with a web site (www.butterscotchlovers.com); my colleague, Kathy Roach, who designed letterhead and mailing labels for my publishing company; Sue Pashko of Envision, who helped guide me through the world of color photography; my daughter, Adria, who, like so many other teenagers, was eager to critique every recipe in the book; and, most of all, my husband, Mario, who though one of the greatest worriers in the world, believed in me enough to let me invest in this self-publishing venture.

Butterscotch Pecan Ice Cream with Hot Butterscotch Sauce (page 34)

Triple Butterscotch Cheesecake (page 32)

Table of Contents

INTRODUCTION

I started teaching myself to cook before I reached my teen years. By the time I was in college, sharing a communal dorm kitchen, I was experimenting with new recipes and helping everyone else in the kitchen make satisfying, nutritious meals. After writing a weekly food column for the *Trenton (NJ) Times* for a number of years, it was only a logical progression to move on to collecting my recipes in a cookbook.

Over the past two decades, I've published several cookbooks—two devoted to cakes (*The Good Cake Book,* New American Library, 1982; *The New Good Cake Book*, W.W. Norton, 1997), one on vegetarian cuisine (*Cashews and Lentils, Apples and Oats,* Contemporary Books, 1981), another on the foods of Lynchburg, Tennessee (*Miss Mary's Down-Home Cooking,* New American Library, 1984), and *New Chocolate Classics* (W.W. Norton, 1999)—wonderful new versions of desserts that had never previously been chocolate.

When the chocolate book had been nearly completed, Lori Gosset, one of my colleagues at work (my non-cookbook career is in public relations) came up to me one day and said, "You know, there are so many foods and cookbooks out there for people who love chocolate, but fans of butterscotch have a lot of trouble finding delicious desserts."

My first response was that there are plenty of sweet butterscotch treats available. In my mind, which is like a computer when it comes to food, I recalled the first butterscotch candy I had ever tasted, as a child of eight. It was imported, with each piece individually wrapped in foil, and so rich and flavorful, I savored piece after piece until the entire package was gone. I remembered a breathtakingly delectable "turtle" sundae I once devoured—with hot butterscotch and fudge sauces liberally poured over icy cold vanilla ice cream and garnished with toasted pecans. And I could almost taste again my first butterscotch blondie. But then my mind drew a blank. Were there, in fact, any other butterscotch desserts?

"Lori," I answered. "I love butterscotch, too. But I'd never be able to come up with enough recipes to create an entire cookbook."

I'm not certain whether Lori has ever been refused a single request in her life. She's one of those amazingly persistent people who continues to badger and argue until you finally give in out of sheer weariness. To be honest, I forget the many points she made in working to convince me to write this book. I do recall phrases like, "There are no other butterscotch cookbooks out there" (which I researched, and she was correct), "There are legions of people who love butterscotch, and their needs aren't being met," and, most persuasive of all, "You are such a creative person, if you put your mind to it, I'm sure you can come up with plenty of butterscotch recipes."

Somewhat reluctantly at first, I took on the challenge and began to seriously consider how I might create a butterscotch cookbook. The first question I had to answer was, what exactly is butterscotch?

What is Butterscotch?

Surprisingly, butterscotch is made of only two primary ingredients—butter and brown sugar. But butterscotch is a rather amazing food that tastes far more wonderful than the sum of its parts. Butterscotch isn't the only food in which basic ingredients are literally transformed through a physical process. Think, for example, of heavy cream being churned into butter, or strawberry preserves, which are remarkably different from just the simple fruit and sugar that went into the cooking pot. So it is with butterscotch. Somehow, when butter is melted and brown sugar is added—in a process that only a physicist could fully explain—butterscotch is the splendid result.

Most people, including me before I started my research, don't realize how frequently butterscotch flavor—in the form of brown sugar and butter—is added to commonly enjoyed foods. Beyond the readily found butterscotch candy, pudding, and ice cream topping, other desserts also containing an abundance of butter and brown sugar include blondies (golden brownies), the topping on apple crisp and certain crumb cakes (if you're like me, you prefer the topping to the actual dessert), pecan pie, etc.

At the grocery store, you'll find a number of foods labeled as "butterscotch," even though they contain little or no butter or brown sugar. These foods rely on artificial flavorings to achieve a taste similar to real butterscotch. If you think you like butterscotch pudding from a mix, wait till you taste the real thing (page 24), which is almost as easy as from a box, but has an incomparably better flavor.

HOW TO GET BUTTERSCOTCH FLAVOR INTO DESSERTS

If you look in almost any dessert cookbook, you'll find lots of recipes that contain butter and brown sugar, including pineapple upside down cake, oatmeal cookies, apple brown betty, even toll-house cookies. The reason why most of these desserts aren't immediately identifiable as butterscotch is that the tastes of the other ingredients are so powerful, the butterscotch flavor plays second fiddle.

In creating recipes for this book, my goal has been to highlight the butterscotch flavor, with other ingredients adding a subtle interplay of tastes but never masking the butterscotch. I've also added butterscotch to the recipes, something that took quite a bit of experimentation to achieve.

When a baker wants to make a chocolate cake, for example, he or she can add cocoa or melted chocolate and voila!: you have a chocolate cake. But how do you add butterscotch? There's only a certain amount of butter and brown sugar that any recipe can contain before it becomes too sweet and rich.

After much trial and error, I found that if I added finely ground butterscotch candy, it would melt into the dessert and impart an intense butterscotch flavor. What's more, the candy blended into the dessert as fully as any other ingredient, so the final result was not at all candy-like.

Sources for Butterscotch Ingredients

HARD BUTTERSCOTCH CANDY

I learned the hard way that you can't grind butterscotch candy in advance of preparing the recipe. This candy quickly absorbs moisture from the air, so within a couple of hours (and sooner on a humid day), the pieces will stick together into a single, unusable lump. The best way to avoid this is to immediately mix the ground butterscotch with another dry ingredient called for in the recipe, such as flour.

Now, the question is, what brand of butterscotch candy should you use in recipes? The answer is, whichever one you most enjoy eating. Grocery stores offer a wide selection of choices, including Hershey's, Werther's, Callard & Bowser, Keiller, and Brach's (their "Special Treasure Golden Butter Toffee" has a better flavor than the disks actually labeled "butterscotch").

If you're on a quest for wonderful butterscotch, as I have been for years, you can purchase less commonly found brands from mail order sources. The most charming package of butterscotch I've encountered is made by Chambers Candy Co. of England. The 5-ounce tin shows a raised design featuring a quaint English candy shop. And the quality of the butterscotch within is impeccable. These candies are imported into the U.S. by

Christopher Brookes Distinctive Foods. If you can't find the tins, you may purchase a six-pack directly from the importer or call them for the name of the closest store selling them.

Christopher Brookes Distinctive Foods
7229 212th Street S.W., Unit D
Edmonds, Washington 98026-7736
Phone: 425-640-2233
Fax: 425-640-6272
Web site: www.cbdf.com

Another mail-order source of hard butterscotch candy is M-B Candies. Not only does this company make exceptionally good butterscotch, but the cost is lower than many grocery store brands. M-B manufactures several flavors of hard candy, and these are sold in assorted bags at many department stores (often under the store's own label) like Marshall Fields and Bloomingdale's. But no store carries bags of only butterscotch candies, so you may wish to order them directly from the manufacturer.

Rucker's Makin' Batch
P.O. Box 27
Bridgeport, Illinois 62417
Phone: 888-MBCANDY (888-622-2639)
E-mail: www.makingbatch.com

In addition, you can easily make your own fine butterscotch (page 88) to enjoy on its own or incorporate into recipes.

BUTTERSCOTCH ICE CREAM TOPPING

Some recipes in this book rely on butterscotch ice cream topping as a means of achieving a true butterscotch flavor. Unfortunately, supermarkets generally sell only low-fat or fat-free versions of topping, which will not work properly in the recipes. The most convenient source for high quality butterscotch ice cream topping is a good ice cream parlor, where you can buy it by the pint. Or, you can make your own (page 34).

With this brief explanation, you now know everything you need to about how to incorporate one of the world's favorite flavors into a variety of recipes. All that remains is to pick which dessert you want to prepare first, and enjoy!

Pies and Baked Fruit Desserts

Butterscotch Crumb Pie

This is a rich, custardy pie with a cookie-like crust and a filling that contains butterscotch brownie crumbs (see recipe for Classic Blondies, page 48).
Note: If more convenient, bake the blondies a day or so in advance of making the pie.

BUTTERSCOTCH COOKIE PIE CRUST

6	tablespoons butter, softened
3	tablespoons dark brown sugar
I	egg
$\frac{1}{2}$	teaspoon vanilla
$\frac{1}{8}$	teaspoon salt
I	cup flour
$\frac{1}{4}$	cup finely crushed butterscotch candy

FILLING

I	cup dark brown sugar
$\frac{1}{2}$	cup water
3	eggs, beaten
I	cup coarsely grated crumbs from Classic Blondies (page 48)
$\frac{1}{3}$	cup flour
$\frac{1}{2}$	teaspoon cinnamon
$5\frac{1}{3}$	tablespoons butter, softened

BUTTERSCOTCH COOKIE PIE CRUST

1. In a large bowl, cream the butter with the brown sugar, continuing to beat until the sugar is completely incorporated. Beat in the egg, vanilla, and salt. Add the flour and beat or stir just until it is incorporated into the dough. Stir in the butterscotch candy.

2. Form the dough into a ball and chill for 30 minutes.

3. Preheat the oven to 375° F.

4. On a lightly floured surface, roll out the dough to fit into a deep 9-inch pie plate. Lay the dough in the pie plate, and prick it all over with the tines of a fork.

5. Bake the crust 10 minutes or until lightly browned. Place the pie plate on a rack to cool while preparing the filling. Lower the oven to 375° F.

FILLING

6 Place the brown sugar, water and beaten eggs in the top of a double boiler over boiling water. Cook, stirring occasionally, until thick. Remove the pot from the heat and let cool slightly.

7 Pour the filling into the pie shell.

8 In a small mixing bowl, stir together the blondie crumbs, flour, and cinnamon. Using your fingertips or two knives, cut in the butter until it is incorporated. Sprinkle the crumb mixture over the filling.

9 Bake the pie 25 minutes. The filling will be set and the topping browned. Transfer the pie to a rack to cool. Serve at room temperature. Refrigerate any leftover pie.

Yield: *10 to 12 servings*

Pecan Pie

If you love butterscotch and adore pecan pie, this is guaranteed to be the best pecan pie you've ever tasted! The crust is cookie-like, with a faint butterscotch flavor. And the filling is chock full of pecans and butterscotch morsels. It's positively addictive.

BROWN SUGAR PIE CRUST

- 1   cup flour
- 2   tablespoons dark brown sugar
- $1/4$ teaspoon salt
- 6   tablespoons butter
- 1   egg yolk
- 1   tablespoon water
- $1/2$ teaspoon vanilla

FILLING

- $1/2$ stick (4 tablespoons) butter, softened
- 1   cup dark brown sugar
- 3   eggs
- $1/2$ cup dark corn syrup
- 1   cup coarsely chopped pecans
- $1/2$ cup butterscotch morsels

BROWN SUGAR PIE CRUST

1 In a mixing bowl, stir together the flour, brown sugar, and salt. Using your fingertips, two knives, or a pastry cutter, work in the butter until the mixture has the consistency of coarse meal. Add the egg yolk, water, and vanilla, and mix until the dough holds together. Form the dough into a ball and chill 30 minutes.

2 Preheat the oven to 400° F.

3 Roll out the dough to fit into a 9-inch pie plate. Place the dough in the pie plate, and prick all over with the tines of a fork. Bake about 7 minutes. The crust will be slightly browned but not completely done. Transfer the pie plate to a rack.

4 Lower the oven to 350° F.

FILLING

5 In a mixing bowl, cream the butter with the brown sugar, beating until the sugar is completely incorporated. Beat in the eggs, then the corn syrup. Stir in the pecans and butterscotch morsels.

6 Pour the filling into the pie shell. Bake about 40 to 45 minutes. The filling will not be completely set, but it will be golden brown in color, and a toothpick inserted about 1 inch from the center will come out clean. Transfer the pie to a rack to cool.

Yield: *10 servings*

Butterscotch-Pecan Tassies

These delectable miniature pies have a meltingly delicious butterscotch-cream cheese crust and a heavenly pecan filling. They are completely irresistible!
Note: This recipe makes 30 miniature pecan pies, which need to be baked in miniature muffin pans. They are most easily removed from the pans if you use miniature foil muffin cup liners.

CREAM CHEESE PASTRY CRUST

7	tablespoons butter, softened
1	3-ounce package cream cheese, softened
$1/2$	cup ground butterscotch candy
1	cup flour
3	butterscotch morsels per muffin cup (about $1/4$ cup morsels)

FILLING

$3/4$	cup dark brown sugar
1	egg
1	tablespoon butter, softened
1	teaspoon vanilla
1	pinch salt
$1/3$	cup chopped pecans

1 Place foil muffin cup liners in 30 miniature muffin cups. (Miniature muffin tins usually contain 12 cups, so if you don't have three pans, you will need to bake the tassies in batches.)

2 Preheat the oven to 350° F.

CREAM CHEESE PASTRY CRUST

3 In a medium bowl, beat together the butter and cream cheese. Beat in the butterscotch candy, then the flour.

4 With lightly floured hands, press small portions of dough on the bottom and up the sides of each muffin cup liner. Drop 3 butterscotch morsels into each cup.

FILLING

5 In another bowl, beat together the brown sugar, egg, butter, vanilla, and salt. Spoon about a teaspoon of filling over the butterscotch morsels, filling the cups almost to the top. Sprinkle with a few pecan pieces.

6 Bake the tassies 25 to 30 minutes, or until the filling is set and the crust is browned. Transfer the pies to a rack to cool.

Yield: 30 miniature pies

Apple-Cranberry-Pecan Pie

This wonderful dessert is like a cross between a pie and a baked fruit crisp. A rich butterscotch cookie crust is covered with a mixture of sautéed apples, dried cranberries, and pecans and then sprinkled with an oatmeal-streusel topping. The pie makes a fine contribution to any holiday feast.

1 Preheat the oven to 375° F.

CRUST

2 Prepare as directed on page 10 (steps 1, 5 and 6). Prick the crust several times with the tines of a fork. Bake about 8 to 10 minutes, or until just very lightly browned. Transfer the crust to a rack. Lower the oven temperature to 325° F.

FILLING

3 Melt the butter in a large skillet. Add the apples and cook, stirring frequently, until just beginning to soften. Remove the pan from the heat and add the flour, then the brown sugar, cranberries, pecans, and cinnamon. Mix gently but thoroughly. Spread the apple filling evenly in the crust.

TOPPING

4 In a medium bowl, stir together the oats, flour, and brown sugar. With a pastry cutter, two knives, or your fingertips, work in the butter until the mixture resembles coarse meal. Stir in the butterscotch morsels.

5 Sprinkle the topping over the filling, and press down gently. Using a knife, cut 3 large slits for steam to escape. Bake the pie 40 to 45 minutes, or until the topping is browned and the filling is bubbly. Transfer to a rack to cool. Serve the pie slightly warm or at room temperature.

Yield: 10 to 12 servings

CRUST

Follow recipe for crust of Butterscotch Streusel Apple Sour Cream Pie (page 10)

FILLING

3	tablespoons butter
6	Granny Smith or other pie apples, peeled, cored, and sliced
2	tablespoons flour
$3/4$	cup dark brown sugar
$3/4$	cup dried cranberries
$1/4$	cup chopped pecans
$1\,1/2$	teaspoons cinnamon

TOPPING

$1/2$	cup rolled oats
$1/4$	cup flour
$1/4$	cup dark brown sugar
$1/2$	stick (4 tablespoons) butter
$2\,1/2$	tablespoons butterscotch morsels

Classic Apple Pie

for Butterscotch Lovers

This is a perfect apple pie: the crust is crisp, rich and delicate, with an apple filling that positively melts in your mouth. The pie has a special twist, though: the crust contains ground butterscotch candy, and the filling a sprinkling of butterscotch morsels. The added flavor is subtle but most definite and welcome.

BUTTERSCOTCH PIE CRUST

- 2 cups flour
- 1 teaspoon salt
- $2/3$ cup ground butterscotch candy
- $1 1/2$ sticks (12 tablespoons) butter, cut into small pieces
- 5 tablespoons ice water

FILLING

- $1/2$ cup dark brown sugar
- $1/8$ teaspoon salt
- 1 tablespoon cornstarch
- $1/4$ teaspoon cinnamon
- 6 Granny Smith, or other pie apples peeled, cored, and thinly sliced
- $1 1/2$ tablespoons butter, cut into very small pieces
- $1/3$ cup butterscotch morsels

BUTTERSCOTCH PIE CRUST

1 In a large bowl, stir together the flour, salt, and butterscotch candy. With a pastry cutter, two knives, or your fingertips, work in the butter until the mixture resembles coarse meal. Add just enough ice water to be able to form the dough into a ball. Chill the dough for 1 to 2 hours.

2 Lightly grease a deep 9-inch or 10-inch pie plate.

3 Divide the dough into two balls, one using nearly $2/3$ of the dough. Roll the larger portion of dough about 3 inches larger than the bottom of the pie plate, and transfer it to the pie plate. (Refrigerate the remaining dough while preparing the filling.)

4 Preheat the oven to 425° F.

FILLING

5 In a large bowl, stir together the brown sugar, cornstarch, salt, and cinnamon, being certain to break up any lumps of sugar or cornstarch. As you slice each apple, add the slices to the bowl, and toss well, coating each slice with the sugar mixture.

6 When all the apples have been sliced, spread the mixture evenly in the pie plate. Sprinkle with the pieces of butter, then the butterscotch morsels.

7 On a lightly floured surface, roll out the remaining ball of dough large enough to cover the top of the pie plate. Transfer to the pie plate, and crimp the edges to seal. Cut 5 large slits in the top crust to allow steam to escape.

8 Place the pie in the oven, and let it bake for 10 minutes. Reduce the heat to 350° F and continue baking for about 40 minutes, or until the crust is browned, and the filling is bubbly. Transfer the pie to a rack to cool. Serve warm or at room temperature.

Yield: *8 to 10 servings*

Butterscotch Streusel
Apple Sour Cream Pie

BUTTERSCOTCH PASTRY CRUST

1	cup flour
$1/3$	cup finely ground butterscotch candy
$1/2$	teaspoon salt
6	tablespoons cold butter
3	tablespoons ice water, approximately

FILLING

1	cup sour cream
$1/3$	cup dark brown sugar
3	tablespoons flour
$1 1/2$	teaspoons vanilla
$1/2$	teaspoon cinnamon
$1/2$	cup buttercotch morsels
6	Granny Smith or other pie apples, peeled, cored and thinly sliced

TOPPING

$1/2$	cup flour
$1/2$	cup dark brown sugar
$1/2$	teaspoon cinnamon
6	tablespoons cold butter, cut into small pieces
$1/2$	cup chopped pecans

Here's a very different recipe for apple pie—one that combines several different textures to produce a spectacularly delicious dessert. The crust is delicate and flavored with butterscotch candy, while the filling contains apples, butterscotch morsels, and sour cream—all topped with a buttery, pecan-crunch streusel.

BUTTERSCOTCH PASTRY CRUST

1 In a bowl, stir together the flour, salt, and butterscotch candy. With a pastry cutter, two knives, or your fingertips, cut in the butter until the mixture resembles coarse meal. Add the water. If necessary, add more water, just until the crust holds together. Chill the crust while preparing the filling and topping.

FILLING

2 In a large bowl, stir together the sour cream, brown sugar, flour, vanilla, and cinnamon. Stir in the butterscotch morsels. As you slice each apple, add the slices to the bowl, and toss to coat with the filling. When all apples have been added, set the mixture aside.

TOPPING

3 In a small bowl, stir together the flour, brown sugar, and cinnamon. Add the butter and, using your fingertips, rub it in until the mixture is crumbly. Add the pecans.

ASSEMBLY & BAKING

4 Preheat the oven to 375° F.

5 Grease a 9-inch pie plate.

6 On a lightly floured surface, roll out the crust to a round about 13 inches in diameter. Fit into the pie plate. Fold any overhanging crust, and crimp the edges.

7 Mound the apple and sour cream mixture in the crust, pressing down lightly to make an even layer. Sprinkle with the topping mixture.

8 Place a baking sheet under the pie plate to catch any drips as the pie bakes. Bake the pie for 1 hour or until bubbly and browned. Transfer to a rack to cool. Serve the pie warm or at room temperature.

Yield: *10 servings*

Butterscotch Apple Crostata

Crostata, an Italian dessert, is like a fruit tart, except that it is made with a cookie dough, rather than a pastry crust, and the filling is not runny. It's similar to a giant fruit-filled cookie and is unbelievably delicious.
*Note: **The top of the crostata is decorated with cookie cut-outs. These can be as simple as circles, or they can match any occasion (e.g., leaves for fall, bunnies for spring, Christmas shapes, etc.).***

FILLING

5	medium Granny Smith or other pie apples, peeled, cored, and cut into $1/4$" slices
3	tablespoons butter
$1/3$	cup dark brown sugar
$1/4$	cup water
$1/3$	cup butterscotch morsels

COOKIE CRUST

2	sticks (1 cup) butter, softened
$1/2$	cup dark brown sugar
1	egg
1	tablespoon vanilla
3	cups flour
$1/4$	teaspoon salt
$1/2$	cup finely ground butterscotch candy

FILLING

1 Place the apple slices, butter, brown sugar, and water in a skillet. Cook, stirring occasionally, about 15 minutes, or until the apples are tender. With a slotted spoon, transfer the apples to a bowl. Cook the liquid remaining in the skillet until thick and caramel-like, about 5 minutes. Pour over the apples. Chill the filling until it is no longer hot, about 30 minutes. Stir in the butterscotch morsels.

COOKIE CRUST

2 In a large bowl, cream the butter with the brown sugar, continuing to beat until the sugar is completely incorporated. Beat in the egg and vanilla.

3 In another bowl, stir together the flour, salt, and butterscotch candy. Add to the creamed mixture, and beat or stir until the dry ingredients are incorporated. Divide the dough into 2 portions, one about twice as large as the other. Place the smaller portion of the dough in the freezer to firm up slightly.

ASSEMBLY & BAKING

4 Preheat the oven to 350° F.

5 Grease an 11-inch pie plate or tart pan.

6 With lightly floured fingertips, press the larger piece of dough into the pan, so it covers the bottom and comes up the sides. Spread the apple filling evenly over the crust.

7 Remove the remaining one-third of the dough from the freezer. On a lightly floured board, roll out the dough to $1/4$-inch thick. Cut into 2-inch circles, or other shapes, and arrange decoratively over the fruit.

8 Bake the crostata about 45 minutes, or until the cookie crust is browned. Transfer to a rack to cool.

Yield: *10 to 12 servings*

Butterscotch Peach Cobbler

A cobbler has a filling like a deep-dish fruit pie, but instead of a crust, delectable biscuits are nestled in the filling. This version contains fresh peaches, which are enhanced by the butterscotch sauce that forms almost "like magic" from melted butterscotch morsels. The biscuits on top are also butterscotch flavored.

*Note: **The easiest way to peel peaches is to bring a large pot of water to a boil. Drop in two peaches at a time, and let them sit in the boiling water for 1 minute. Remove with a slotted spoon. Repeat with additional peaches. When the peaches are cool enough to handle, the skin will slip right off.***

FILLING

1 1/2 pounds (about 5 large) fresh ripe peaches, peeled, pitted, and cut into thick slices

2 tablespoons butter, melted

1/2 cup dark brown sugar

2 tablespoons cornstarch

1/2 cup butterscotch morsels

TOPPING

2/3 cup flour

1/4 cup dark brown sugar

1 teaspoon baking powder

1/8 teaspoon salt

2 tablespoons butter

2 1/2 tablespoons milk

2 tablespoons crushed butterscotch candy

1 Grease a deep 9-inch pie plate.

2 Preheat the oven to 375° F.

FILLING

3 In a large bowl, stir together the melted butter, brown sugar, and cornstarch. Add the peaches and butterscotch morsels, and mix well. Spread evenly in the prepared pan.

TOPPING

4 In a bowl, stir together the flour, brown sugar, baking powder, and salt. With a pastry cutter, two knives, or your fingertips, cut in the butter until the mixture resembles coarse meal. Stir in the milk.

5 Turn the dough out onto a lightly floured board. With a rolling pin, roll out the dough to a thickness of about 1/3 inch. Cut into rounds using a 2-inch cookie cutter, and place the rounds evenly over the filling. Sprinkle the biscuit rounds with the butterscotch candy. Any leftover candy can be sprinkled over the filling.

6 Bake the cobbler 30 minutes. The filling will be bubbly and the biscuits browned. Transfer to a rack to cool. The dessert may be served warm or at room temperature.

Yield: *8 servings*

Apple Brown Betty

Apple Brown Betty is an early American dessert and one of the easiest to make, with apple slices alternating with crumbs, sugar, and spices before being baked to a golden delight. This version uses crumbs from Classic Blondies, as well as butterscotch morsels, to enhance the buttery brown sugar taste. The dessert is spectacular served warm from the oven with a scoop of Butterscotch Ice Cream (page 34) or vanilla ice cream.

$1\frac{1}{4}$ coarse crumbs made from Classic Blondies (page 48)

$\frac{1}{3}$ cup dark brown sugar

1 teaspoon cinnamon

$\frac{1}{4}$ teaspoon nutmeg

$2\frac{1}{2}$ pounds apples (about 6 medium), peeled, cored, and sliced

$\frac{1}{2}$ cup butterscotch morsels

$\frac{1}{3}$ cup water

$\frac{1}{2}$ stick (4 tablespoons) butter, cut into small pieces

1 Preheat the oven to 375° F.

2 Grease a 9-inch square pan.

3 In a small bowl, stir together the blondie crumbs, brown sugar, cinnamon, and nutmeg. Sprinkle 2 tablespoons of this mixture in the bottom of the prepared pan.

4 Place half the apple slices evenly in the pan. Sprinkle with half the butterscotch morsels, all the water, one-third of the remaining crumb mixture, and then one-third of the butter bits. Cover with the remaining apple slices, rest of the butterscotch morsels, rest of the crumb mixture, and rest of the butter.

5 Bake the dessert 35 minutes.

Yield: *6 to 8 servings*

Butterscotch Baked Peaches

This dessert allows you to enjoy the freshest fruit of summer, while incorporating the rich flavor of butterscotch. Golden peach slices, when baked, become enveloped in a caramel-like sauce and are topped with a thin crust of delicious cake. The dessert is easy to make and practically fool-proof.

Note: **See page 14 for how to peel peaches.**

1 Preheat the oven to 350° F.

2 Pour the melted butter into the bottom of a 9″ x 13″ baking pan. Arrange the peach slices in an even layer over the butter.

3 In a mixing bowl, stir together the flour, brown sugar, and baking powder until well mixed, breaking up any lumps of sugar with the back of a spoon. Add the milk gradually, stirring after each addition. Stir in the vanilla and butterscotch morsels.

4 Pour the batter evenly over the peaches.

5 Bake the dessert 35 to 40 minutes. Serve warm or at room temperature.

Yield: *15 servings*

1	stick ($1/2$ cup) butter, melted
3	pounds (about 9 large) ripe peaches, peeled and sliced
1	cup flour
1	cup dark brown sugar
1	tablespoon baking powder
$3/4$	cup milk
1	teaspoon vanilla
$1/2$	cup butterscotch morsels
$1/4$	cup ground butterscotch candy

Blueberry Crumble

This dessert is less intensely butterscotch flavored than most of the recipes in the book, which allows the delicious taste of fresh blueberries to come through. The filling for this Crumble is like blueberry pie filling. But instead of a crust, the berries are topped with a delectable butter-pecan-oatmeal topping.

Note: Blueberry Crumble is best served on the day it is made, while still slightly warm from the oven. (Try it topped with a scoop of vanilla or Butterscotch Ice Cream, page 34). Any leftovers must be refrigerated. Reheat in the microwave or conventional oven before serving.

FILLING

1	cup dark brown sugar
2	pints fresh blueberries, washed and picked over
2	teaspoons water
1	teaspoon cornstarch

TOPPING

1	cup rolled oats
1	cup dark brown sugar
$^1/_2$	cup flour
1	cup chopped pecans
1	stick ($^1/_2$ cup) butter

1 Grease a 9" x 13" baking pan.

2 Preheat the oven to 375° F.

FILLING

3 Place the brown sugar in a large bowl. With the back of a spoon, press out any lumps in the sugar. Add the blueberries and toss well. In a small cup, dissolve the cornstarch in the water. Add to the bowl with the blueberries, and toss again. Spread the blueberry mixture evenly in the prepared pan.

TOPPING

4 In another bowl, stir together the oats, brown sugar, flour, and pecans. With a pastry cutter, two knives, or your fingertips, cut in the butter until the mixture is crumbly and the texture of coarse meal. Sprinkle evenly over the blueberries.

5 Bake the crumble 35 minutes. The filling will be bubbly and the top golden brown. Let the dessert cool on a rack for at least 30 minutes before serving.

Yield: *10 to 12 servings*

Apricot Cookie Crumble

Similar to the previous blueberry recipe, this one also contains a luscious fruit filling and baked on topping. The color and fragrance of baked apricots is incredibly lovely, and the dessert is even better when topped with a scoop of vanilla or butterscotch ice cream.

FILLING

$2^{1}/_{4}$ pounds (about 10 large) apricots, pitted and cut into thick slices

$^{3}/_{4}$ cup dark brown sugar

3 tablespoons butterscotch ice cream topping

TOPPING

1 cup rolled oats

$^{3}/_{4}$ cup flour

$^{1}/_{2}$ cup dark brown sugar

$^{1}/_{4}$ teaspoon cinnamon

$^{1}/_{4}$ teaspoon salt

$^{1}/_{2}$ stick (4 tablespoons) butter

1 egg

$1^{1}/_{2}$ tablespooons dark corn syrup

$^{1}/_{2}$ cup chopped pecans

1 Preheat the oven to 375° F.

2 Grease a 9″ x 9″ baking pan.

3 Place the apricots, brown sugar, and butterscotch topping in the baking pan. Toss until well mixed.

TOPPING

4 In a large bowl, stir together the oats, flour, brown sugar, cinnamon, and salt. With a pastry cutter, two knives, or your fingertips, cut in the butter until the mixture resembles coarse meal.

5 In a small bowl, beat together the egg and corn syrup. Add to the oat mixture and stir until crumbly. Drop by teaspoonfuls evenly over the apricot mixture. Sprinkle with the pecans.

6 Bake the dessert for 35 minutes, or until the syrup is bubbly and the topping is browned. Let cool slightly before serving, but serve while still warm.

Yield: 6 to 8 servings

Pineapple Butterscotch Crisp

This special dessert takes a bit more time than most fruit crisps but is definitely worth the extra trouble. A whole, peeled pineapple is first roasted in a caramel-like glaze, then chopped and baked in a casserole with a crunchy, butterscotch topping. When served with a scoop of Butterscotch Graham Swirl Ice Cream (page 34), this dessert is hard to beat.

1 Preheat the oven to 400° F.

2 Grease a shallow 1-quart casserole dish.

PINEAPPLE

3 In a medium saucepan, bring the water and brown sugar to a boil, stirring to dissolve the sugar. Boil the mixture for 5 minutes without stirring. Remove from the heat and add the brandy. Transfer the mixture to a 9-inch square baking pan. Place the pineapple in the pan and bake it about 50 minutes, rotating it in the sauce every 10 minutes.

4 Remove the pineapple from the oven and transfer it to a cutting board. Reduce the oven temperature to 350° F. Cut the pineapple into quarters and remove and discard the core. Cut the flesh into $1/2$-inch cubes and place in the prepared casserole dish. Drizzle $1/3$ cup of the syrup remaining in the baking pan over the pineapple.

TOPPING

5 Place the flour and brown sugar in the container of a food processor fitted with a metal blade. Add the butter and process until the mixture is like coarse meal. Do not over process. Add the pecans and butterscotch morsels, and process until chopped.

6 Sprinkle the topping over the pineapple. Bake about 20 minutes, or until bubbly. Serve warm or at room temperature.

Yield: *6 servings*

PINEAPPLE

1	cup dark brown sugar
$1\,1/2$	cups water
2	tablespoons brandy
1	fresh pineapple, peeled but kept whole

TOPPING

1	cup flour
$1/4$	cup dark brown sugar
6	tablespoons butter, coarsely chopped
$1/3$	cup pecans
$1/3$	cup butterscotch morsels

21

Blueberry "Cheese Cake"

This is a two-layered dessert, with the bottom a thin butterscotch, cream cheese cake. Lots of fresh ripe blueberries inbedded in a lovely, caramel-colored custard form the top layer. It's a wonderfully satisfying dessert that's not overly sweet or rich.

CAKE LAYER

1	stick ($^1/_2$ cup) butter, softened
1	3-ounce package cream cheese, softened
$^1/_2$	cup dark brown sugar
1	egg
1 $^1/_2$	cups flour
1 $^1/_2$	teaspoons baking powder
$^1/_2$	cup ground butterscotch candy

FILLING

2	eggs
2	tablespoons cornstarch
$^1/_2$	cup dark brown sugar
1	teaspoon vanilla
2	8-ounce containers vanilla yogurt
2	pints blueberries, washed and picked over
$^1/_2$	cup butterscotch morsels

CAKE LAYER

1 Grease a 9" x 13" baking pan.

2 Preheat the oven to 350° F.

3 In a large bowl, cream the butter, cream cheese, and brown sugar, continuing to beat until the sugar is fully incorporated. Beat in the egg. Add the flour, baking powder, and ground butterscotch to the bowl, and beat until the dry ingredients are incorporated.

4 Spread the batter evenly in the prepared pan, and set aside.

FILLING

5 In another bowl, beat the eggs. Add the cornstarch and mix until dissolved. Add the brown sugar, vanilla, and yogurt, and beat until well mixed.

6 Sprinkle the blueberries evenly over the cake batter. Top with the butterscotch morsels. Pour the yogurt mixture over the berries, and spread to make an even coating.

7 Bake the dessert for 1 hour. Transfer the pan to a rack to cool. Serve the dessert at room temperature or chilled.

Yield: *15 to 18 serving*

Puddings, Ice Creams

and Other Favorite Butterscotch Desserts

Butterscotch Pudding

Once you try the homemade version, you may never be able to eat pudding from a boxed mix again. This is smooth and creamy, with a wonderful butterscotch flavor.

$\frac{1}{2}$ cup dark brown sugar

3 tablespoons cornstarch

2 cups milk

1 $\frac{1}{2}$ tablespoons butter

3 tablespoons crushed butterscotch candy

1 teaspoon vanilla

1 In a medium saucepan, stir together the brown sugar and cornstarch, breaking up any lumps with the back of the spoon. Add about $\frac{1}{2}$ cup of milk and stir to dissolve the sugar and cornstarch. Add the remaining milk, butter, and butterscotch candy.

2 Cook the mixture over a medium heat, stirring frequently, until the mixture reaches a full boil. Remove from the heat and stir in the vanilla.

3 Pour the pudding into a serving dish or 4 individual dessert bowls. Chill before serving.

Yield: *4 servings*

Souffléd Two-Layer Pudding

This recipe, containing 8 beaten egg whites, rises dramatically in the oven and then falls while cooling to form a two-layered pudding. The bottom layer is thick, dense, and rich, while the top layer is light and airy. Both are deliciously butterscotch flavored.

10 tablespoons butter

6 ounces (about 1 1/4 cups) butterscotch morsels

8 eggs, separated

1 cup dark brown sugar

1/4 cup ground pecans

2 1/2 tablespoons brandy

1 Preheat the oven to 375° F.

2 Grease a tube pan with a removable bottom.

3 Place the butter and butterscotch morsels in a medium saucepan. Cook, stirring often, over a very low heat until melted. Remove from the heat. (The mixture will separate, but this is fine.)

4 In a large bowl, beat the egg whites until stiff. Set aside.

5 In another large bowl, beat the egg yolks. Gradually beat in the brown sugar, continuing to beat until the mixture is thick. Beat in the melted butterscotch mixture, then the pecans and brandy.

6 Stir about one-third of the egg whites into the egg yolk mixture to lighten it. Then fold in the rest of the egg whites, gently but thoroughly. Pour the batter into the prepared pan.

7 Bake the pudding about 30 minutes, or until a toothpick inserted in the highest part of the pudding will comes out clean. Transfer the pudding to a rack to cool. Run a knife around the edges of the pan and the center cone, so when the pudding falls, it will do so evenly. Serve at room temperature or chilled. Cut into wedges to serve.

Yield: *8 to 10 servings*

Butterscotch Pudding-Cake

Pudding-Cake is a baked dessert that's a cross between a rich, gooey pudding and a brownie-textured cake. Usually chocolate flavored, this luscious butterscotch version shouldn't be missed. Serve it warm with a scoop of ice cream.

Pudding-Cake is one of the fastest, easiest desserts to prepare. It takes only one pot for preparing the batter, and all you need is a spoon for the mixing. The dessert is ready for the oven in less than 15 minutes.

1 Preheat the oven to 350° F.

2 Grease a 9″ square baking pan.

3 In a large saucepan, melt the butter. Remove from the heat and stir in the milk, salt, $3/4$ cup brown sugar, and vanilla. Add the flour and baking powder and stir well. Add the butterscotch morsels and pecans.

4 Spread the batter evenly in the prepared pan.

5 Mix together the hot water and remaining 1 cup brown sugar. Gently pour over the batter in the pan.

6 Bake the dessert 35 minutes, or until hot and bubbly. Let cool at least 10 minutes before serving, but serve warm.

Yield: *8 to 10 servings*

$1/2$	stick (4 tablespoons) butter
$1/3$	cup milk
$1/8$	teaspoon salt
$3/4$	cup plus 1 cup dark brown sugar, divided usage
$1 1/2$	teaspoons vanilla
1	cup flour
2	teaspoons baking powder
$1/2$	11-ounce package butterscotch morsels
1	cup chopped pecans
$1 3/4$	cups hot tap water

27

Butter Brittle Bread Pudding

Just about everyone loves bread pudding, and this version is one of the best due to the incomparable flavor of homemade pecan brittle. Once you've made the candy, the pudding itself takes just a few minutes to put together.

Note: If preferred, the pudding can also be baked in a single 2-quart casserole, for about the same length of time.

4	cups French or Italian bread, in $\frac{1}{2}$-inch cubes
4	eggs
$\frac{1}{2}$	cup dark brown sugar
$2\frac{1}{4}$	cups milk
I	tablespoon vanilla
$\frac{1}{2}$	cup butterscotch morsels
I	cup coarsely chopped Nut Brittle (page 90), made with pecans

1 Grease 6 individual baking dishes.

2 Preheat the oven to 350° F.

3 Place the bread cubes on a baking sheet, and bake for 10 minutes, stirring once.

4 While the bread cubes are baking, beat the eggs in a large bowl. Beat in the brown sugar, continuing to beat until the mixture is thick. Stir in the milk, vanilla, butterscotch morsels, and pecan brittle. Add the bread cubes, and stir until moistened.

5 Divide the mixture evenly between the prepared baking dishes, filling them no more than $\frac{2}{3}$ full. Bake for 55 to 60 minutes, or until set. Transfer the dishes to a rack to cool. Serve the pudding warm, at room temperature, or chilled, plain or with whipped cream or ice cream.

Yield: *6 servings*

Death By Butterscotch

Everyone's heard of "Death by Chocolate." This is my version of "Death by Butterscotch" and it is undoubtedly one of the richest recipes in the book. The crust for this pie-like dessert is a buttery shortbread, which is filled with a caramelized pecan-butterscotch mixture reminiscent of pecan pie. Serve the dessert cut into very thin wedges.

FILLING

1   cup sugar
2   tablespoons dark corn syrup
1/4   cup water
2/3   cup heavy or whipping cream, heated to barely warm
1   cup chopped pecans
1   cup butterscotch morsels

BUTTERSCOTCH SHORTBREAD CRUST

3   cups flour
1/2   cup dark brown sugar
1/2   cup finely ground butterscotch candy
2   sticks (1 cup) butter, cut into small pieces
2   egg yolks
1/4   cup heavy or whipping cream

FILLING

1   Place the sugar, corn syrup, and water in a medium saucepan. Cook, stirring frequently, until the sugar is dissolved. Bring the mixture to a boil, and let it boil until it turns a deep amber color.

2   Remove the pan from the heat. Slowly add the cream, stirring as you do so. Add the pecans and return the pan to the heat. Cook, stirring, for 1 minute.

3   Transfer the filling mixture to a bowl and let cool to room temperature. Stir in the butterscotch morsels.

BUTTERSCOTCH SHORTBREAD CRUST

4   In a large bowl, stir together the flour, brown sugar, and ground butterscotch. With a pastry cutter, two knives, or your fingertips, work in the butter until the mixture is like coarse meal. In a small bowl, beat together the egg yolks and heavy cream. Add to the flour mixture and stir until the dry ingredients are moistened. Knead the dough briefly until it forms a ball.

Assembly & Baking

5 Preheat the oven to 350° F.

6 Grease a 10- or 11-inch shallow pie plate.

7 Press a little more than half the dough into the bottom and up the sides of the prepared pie plate. Pour the filling over the crust. Roll out the remaining dough between two sheets of waxed paper to a 10- or 11-inch circle (depending on the size of your pie plate) and fit over the filling. Crimp the edges with the tines of a fork. Prick the top all over with the fork to let steam escape.

8 Bake the dessert for 40 minutes, or until golden brown. About halfway through the baking, remove the dessert from the oven and re-prick the top with a fork. (This is necessary because the original holes may close during baking, and the steam will not be able to escape.)

9 Transfer the dessert to a rack to cool. Serve slightly warm or at room temperature.

Yield: *16 servings*

Triple Butterscotch
Cheesecake

Everything you ever wanted in a cheesecake—rich, dense, and creamy—but with the bonus of butterscotch. This is an exceptionally quick and easy cheesecake to prepare.

GRAHAM CRACKER CRUST

18   square graham crackers, crushed

$1/4$ cup dark brown sugar

$1/3$ cup ($5 1/3$ tablespoons) butter, melted

$1/2$ cup chopped pecans

$1/2$ cup butterscotch morsels

FILLING

2   8-ounce packages cream cheese, softened

$1/4$ cup dark brown sugar

2   eggs

2   teaspoons vanilla

$1/3$ cup crushed butterscotch candy

3   tablespoons butterscotch ice cream topping

1   Grease a 9-inch deep dish pie plate.

2   Preheat the oven to 325° F.

GRAHAM CRACKER CRUST

3   Stir together the crushed grahams, brown sugar, and melted butter. Press evenly into the bottom and sides of the prepared pan. Sprinkle with the pecans and butterscotch morsels.

FILLING

4   In a large bowl, beat the cream cheese with the brown sugar until the mixture is smooth. Beat in the eggs and vanilla, then the butterscotch candy.

5   Pour the filling into the crust. Bake the cheesecake 45 minutes. Remove from the oven and let cool on a rack to room temperature. Drizzle the butterscotch topping over the cheesecake and swirl attractively. Chill until very cold, at least 4 hours.

Yield: *12 servings*

Butterscotch Pecan Ice Cream
with Hot Butterscotch Sauce

This is a heavenly dessert. The ice cream itself—a rich butter pecan—is wonderful served alone. But when bathed in a hot butterscotch sauce, it becomes truly ethereal.

ICE CREAM

- 4 tablespoons butter, divided usage
- $3/4$ cup coarsely chopped pecans
- $3/4$ cup brown sugar
- $1/2$ cup milk
- 2 cups (1 pint) heavy or whipping cream
- pinch salt
- $1/2$ cup pasturized egg product (such as Egg Beaters)
- $1/2$ cup finely chopped butterscotch candy

HOT BUTTERSCOTCH SAUCE

- $1/3$ cup dark corn syrup
- $2/3$ cup dark brown sugar
- $2 1/2$ tablespoons butter
- $1/8$ teaspoon salt
- $1/3$ cup milk
- $1/2$ cup pecan halves, optional

ICE CREAM

1 Melt 2 tablespoons butter in a small skillet. Add the pecans and cook, stirring frequently, until golden brown. Transfer to a paper towel to cool.

2 Place the sugar, milk, and remaining 2 tablespoons butter in a saucepan. Cook, stirring often, until the butter has melted and the sugar dissolves. Remove from the heat and let cool slightly. Stir in the cream, salt, and egg product. Chill several hours or until cold.

3 Freeze the ice cream in an ice cream maker according to the manufacturer's instructions. When almost frozen, add the pecans and butterscotch candy. When completely frozen, remove from the ice cream maker and place in a freezer container. Freeze until ready to serve.

HOT BUTTERSCOTCH SAUCE

4 Place the corn syrup, sugar, butter, and salt in a saucepan. Bring to a boil, stirring often. Continue boiling a few minutes, or until the mixture is smooth. Remove from the heat and add the milk and optional pecans. Serve immediately over ice cream, or chill for later use and reheat before serving.

Yield: *$1 1/2$ pints ice cream*
1 cup sauce

Graham Swirl Ice Cream

This is a wonderfully smooth and rich ice cream. The ice cream base is primarily vanilla, with a faint hint of butterscotch from the addition of brown sugar. The real butterscotch flavor comes from ice cream topping that's mixed with chopped graham crackers, which absorb the topping to become soft, moist and delectably flavored.

Note: The mixture for the ice cream base should be prepared several hours in advance to allow it to thoroughly chill and to let the brown sugar fully dissolve. In addition, the grahams should be mixed with the butterscotch topping several hours in advance to chill and absorb the topping.

$1/2$ cup pastured egg product, such as Egg Beaters

$3/4$ cup dark brown sugar

I cup milk

I pint heavy or whipping cream

I teaspoon vanilla

I cup coarsely chopped graham crackers

$1/2$ cup butterscotch ice cream topping

1 In a pitcher or a bowl with a spout, beat the egg product with the brown sugar. Stir in the milk, heavy cream, and vanilla. Cover and let sit in the refrigerator several hours, until very cold.

2 In a small bowl, stir together the graham crackers and topping. Cover and place in the refrigerator several hours.

3 Freeze the ice cream in an ice cream maker according to the manufacturer's directions. When nearly frozen, add the graham crackers. The crackers will be stuck together. You can either scoop out $1/2$-inch balls with a spoon. Or, transfer the mixture to a cutting board and chop it coarsely before adding to the ice cream. Continue processing the ice cream until the grahams have been mixed in.

4 Transfer the mixture to a freezer container, and freeze the ice cream until ready to serve.

Yield: *2 quarts*

Butterscotch Cookies and Bars

Slice-and-Bake Cookies

Almost as easy to prepare as the Slice-And-Bake Cookies you buy at the supermarket, these are far better. A day (or more) in advance, you prepare the dough. Then, when you want cookies, you just slice and bake—it's that simple.

The flavor of these cookies is incomparable—a rich butterscotch taste embedded in a crispy butter wafer.

$\frac{1}{2}$ cup (1 stick) butter, softened

$1\frac{1}{4}$ cups dark brown sugar

1 egg

1 teaspoon vanilla

$1\frac{1}{2}$ cups flour

$1\frac{1}{2}$ teaspoons baking powder

$\frac{1}{8}$ teaspoon salt

$\frac{1}{2}$ cup chopped almonds

2 to 3 tablespoons finely crushed butterscotch candy

1 In a large bowl, cream the butter with the brown sugar, continuing to beat until the sugar is fully incorporated. Beat in the egg and vanilla.

2 In another bowl, stir together the flour, baking powder, and salt. Add to the creamed mixture, beating or stirring until the dry ingredients are incorporated. Stir in the almonds.

3 Form the dough into a 2-inch wide roll on a piece of plastic wrap. Cover the dough completely with the plastic, and chill 24 hours.

4 Preheat the oven to 375° F.

5 Grease one or more cookie sheets. (You will need 3 cookie sheets for this amount of dough, or the cookies can be baked in batches.)

6 With a sharp knife, cut the roll of dough into $\frac{1}{4}$-inch slices. Place the slices on the cookie sheet, allowing at least $1\frac{1}{2}$ inches between each slice for spreading. Sprinkle the tops of the cookies with the crushed butterscotch, and press down lightly.

7 Bake the cookies 8 to 9 minutes, or until lightly browned. Transfer to a rack to cool.

Yield: *38 to 40 cookies*

Butterscotch Chip Cookies

Just like classic toll house cookies—rich, soft, and chewy—but with butterscotch chips instead of chocolate. Adding crushed butterscotch candy to the batter enhances the flavor.

1	stick ($\frac{1}{2}$ cup) butter, softened
1	cup dark brown sugar
1	egg
$\frac{1}{2}$	teaspoon vanilla
1 $\frac{1}{4}$	cups flour
$\frac{1}{3}$	cup crushed butterscotch candy
$\frac{1}{2}$	teaspoon baking powder
$\frac{1}{8}$	teaspoon salt
$\frac{1}{3}$	cup chopped pecans
$\frac{1}{3}$	cup butterscotch morsels

1 Preheat the oven to 350° F.

2 Grease 2 cookie sheets. (If you only have one sheet, you may bake the cookies in batches.)

3 In a large bowl, cream the butter with the brown sugar, continuing to beat until the sugar is fully incorporated. Beat in the egg, then the vanilla.

4 In a small bowl, stir together the flour, butterscotch candy, baking powder, and salt. Add to the creamed mixture, beating or stirring until the dry ingredients are incorporated. Stir in the pecans and butterscotch morsels.

5 Using a tablespoon, drop the batter in 2-inch mounds on the prepared sheet. Make sure to leave a couple of inches between each mound for the cookies to spread while baking.

6 Bake the cookies about 13 minutes, or until lightly browned. Transfer to a rack to cool.

Yield: *18 cookies*

Oatmeal Scotchies

These cookies disappeared so quickly, I almost didn't get to sample them myself! They are big, chewy oatmeal cookies, filled with butterscotch chips and pecans.

1	stick ($^1/_2$ cup) butter, softened
1$^1/_4$	cups dark brown sugar
1	egg
1	tablespoon milk
1	teaspoon vanilla
1	cup flour
1	cup rolled oats
$^1/_2$	cup coarsely ground butterscotch candy
$^1/_2$	teaspoon baking soda
$^1/_2$	teaspoon baking powder
$^1/_2$	cup butterscotch morsels
$^1/_2$	cup chopped pecans

1 Preheat the oven to 350° F.

2 Grease one or more cookie sheets. (You will need three sheets for this recipe, or the cookies may be baked in batches.)

3 In a large bowl, cream the butter with the brown sugar, continuing to beat until the sugar is fully incorporated. Beat in the egg, milk, and vanilla.

4 In another bowl, stir together the flour, oats, butterscotch candy, baking soda, and baking powder. Add to the creamed mixture, beating or stirring until the dry ingredients are incorporated. Stir in the butterscotch morsels and pecans.

5 Using a tablespoon, drop the batter into mounds, about 2$^1/_2$ inches across, onto the cookie sheet. Allow plenty of room for the cookies to spread while baking.

6 Bake about 15 minutes or until lightly browned. Transfer to a rack to cool.

Yield: *18 large cookies*

Crunchy Wholegrain
Butterscotch Cookies

These cookies are unbelievably addictive! They're crunchy and crumbly at the same time,
so it's almost impossible to keep from breaking off another little piece, then another,
and yet another...It's hard to imagine that a batch of these cookies would last long in
anyone's house.

1 Preheat the oven to 350° F.

2 Grease one or more cookie sheets, line the sheets with parchment paper, and lightly coat the paper with non-stick spray. (These cookies are too delicate to bake directly on the cookie sheets; if you do, they will be difficult to remove without breaking.)

3 In a large bowl, cream the butter with the brown sugar, continuing to beat until the sugar is fully incorporated. Beat in the egg and vanilla.

4 In another bowl, stir together the flour, oats, Grape-Nuts, butterscotch candy, and baking powder. Add to the creamed mixture and beat or stir until the dry ingredients are incorporated. The dough will be very stiff. Stir in the butterscotch morsels.

5 With lightly floured hands, break off a piece of dough and roll it into a ball about $1^1/_2$-inches in diameter. Place on the prepared cookie sheet. Continue forming cookies, placing them at least an inch apart to allow room for spreading.

6 Bake the cookies in batches for about 15 minutes, or until browned. Slide the paper off the cookie sheet onto the kitchen counter. Let the cookies sit a few minutes until firm before removing from the paper. Let cool completely on a rack.

Yield: *$3^1/_2$ to 4 dozen cookies*

2	sticks (1 cup) butter, softened
1	cup dark brown sugar
1	egg
1	teaspoon vanilla
1	cup whole wheat flour
$1^1/_2$	cups rolled oats
$1^1/_2$	cups Grape-Nuts or similar cereal
$^1/_2$	cup coarsely ground butterscotch candy
1	teaspoon baking powder
1	cup butterscotch morsels

Thumbprint Cookies

Thumbprint cookies are rich and buttery, and generally filled with an assortment of jams. They get their name from the hole that is made in the top of the cookie, presumably with your thumb, for the jam. In this version of thumbprint cookies, butterscotch ice cream topping replaces the jam, with wonderful results.

l	stick ($\frac{1}{2}$ cup) butter, softened
l	cup dark brown sugar
2	eggs, one of them separated
l	teaspoon vanilla
2	cups flour
$\frac{1}{3}$	cup crushed butterscotch candy
$\frac{1}{8}$	teaspoon salt
$\frac{1}{4}$	cup butterscotch ice cream topping

1 Preheat the oven to 375° F.

2 Grease two cookie sheets (or bake the cookies in batches).

3 In a large bowl, cream the butter with the brown sugar, continuing to beat until the sugar is fully incorporated. Beat in the whole egg and one egg yolk. (Reserve the egg white in a small bowl.) Beat in the vanilla.

4 In another bowl, stir together the flour, butterscotch candy, and salt. Add to the creamed mixture, beating or stirring until the dry ingredients are incorporated.

5 With lightly floured hands, pinch off a 1-inch diameter round piece of dough. Roll between your palms to make a smooth ball. Dip in the egg white, and place on the prepared baking sheet. Repeat with the remaining dough.

6 Bake the cookies 5 minutes. Remove the baking sheets from he oven. With the end of the handle of a wooden spoon, poke a deep hole in the center of each cookie. (First, dip the handle in flour to prevent it from sticking in the cookies.) When all the cookies have holes, fill each with about $\frac{1}{4}$ teaspoon butterscotch ice cream topping.

7 Return the cookies to the oven and continue baking until lightly browned, about 8 minutes more. Transfer the cookies to a rack to cool.

Yield: *About 2 dozen 2$\frac{1}{2}$-inch cookies*

Lori's Butterscotch Biscotti

This recipe was first published in **The New Good Cake Book** *(Dalsass, W.W. Norton, 1997)*
and was the original recipe I developed for my butterscotch-loving friend, who was the
inspiration for an entire book dedicated to this flavor.

1 Preheat the oven to 350° F.

2 Grease a large baking sheet.

3 In a large bowl, beat the eggs. Gradually beat in the brown sugar, continuing to beat until the mixture is thick and pale. Beat in the melted butter, then the vanilla and water.

4 In another bowl, stir together the flour, baking powder, and salt. Add to the egg mixture, stirring until the dry ingredients are incorporated. Stir in the pecans and butterscotch morsels.

5 On the prepared baking sheet, form the dough into two logs, each about 13″ x $2^1/_2$″. Bake the logs for 30 minutes.

6 Remove the baking sheet from the oven, and reduce the oven temperature to 300° F. Cut each log on the diagonal into about 10 slices. Lay the slices on their side, and bake the biscotti for 15 minutes. Turn the slices over, and bake 10 minutes longer or until lightly browned. Transfer the biscotti to a rack to cool.

Yield: *about 20 biscotti*

2	eggs
1	cup dark brown sugar
1	stick ($^1/_2$ cup) butter, melted
2	teaspoons vanilla
2	tablespoons water
3	cups flour
2	teaspoons baking powder
$^1/_4$	teaspoon salt
$^1/_2$	cup chopped pecans
1	6-ounce package butterscotch morsels

Classic Blondies

These have the texture of moist, rich brownies, but are butterscotch flavored—in fact, even more so than usual, with the addition of ground butterscotch candy.
Variation: **When the bars have cooled (before cutting them), spread with $1/3$ cup butterscotch ice cream topping. Sprinkle with $1/2$ cup finely chopped pecans mixed with $1/3$ cup finely chopped butterscotch morsels. Press down lightly. Cut into bars.**

1	cup (2 sticks) butter, softened
1	cup dark brown sugar
2	eggs
2	teaspoons vanilla
$2^{1}/_{2}$	cups flour
$2/_{3}$	cup finely ground hard butterscotch candy
1	teaspoon baking soda
$1/_{4}$	teaspoon salt
1	cup butterscotch chips, chopped pecans, or half of each

1 Preheat the oven to 375° F.

2 Grease a 9" x 13" baking pan.

3 In a large bowl, cream together the butter and brown sugar, continuing to beat until the sugar is completely incorporated. Beat in the eggs and vanilla.

4 In another bowl, stir together the flour, ground butterscotch, baking soda, and salt. Add to the creamed mixture, beating or stirring until the dry ingredients are incorporated. Stir in the butterscotch chips and/or pecans.

5 Spread the batter evenly in the prepared pan. Bake the bars 20 to 25 minutes, or until lightly browned and a toothpick inserted in the center comes out clean. Transfer the pan to a rack to cool. Cut into bars when cool.

Yield: *30 blondies*

Pecan-Filled Italian Cookies

Not too sweet, unbelievably delicate, with just a hint of butterscotch flavor, these cookies smack of the "Old World." The filling—a thick mixture of ground pecans and brown sugar—is encased in a rich, buttery cookie dough.

FILLING

8	ounces (about $1^3/_4$ cups) pecans
1	cup dark brown sugar
1	cup water
$^1/_4$	teaspoon cinnamon

DOUGH

$2^1/_4$	cups flour
$^1/_2$	cup dark brown sugar
$^1/_3$	cup ground butterscotch candy
2	teaspoons baking powder
1	stick ($^1/_2$ cup) butter
1	egg, beaten
6	tablespoons milk

FILLING

1 In a food processor, grind the pecans with the brown sugar until the nuts are finely ground. Transfer to a medium-size, heavy saucepan. Add the water and cinnamon. Bring the mixture to a boil, stirring occasionally. Lower the heat, so the mixture remains at a bare simmer. Cook, uncovered, stirring occasionally, until the mixture is thick, about 30 minutes. Remove from the heat and let cool completely before proceeding with the recipe.

2 Preheat the oven to 350° F.

3 Grease 1 or more cookie sheets.

Dough

4 In a large bowl, stir together the flour, brown sugar, butterscotch candy, and baking powder. With a pastry cutter, two knives, or your fingertips, work in the butter until the mixture resembles coarse meal. Mix together the beaten egg and the milk. Add to the flour mixture, and mix until a smooth dough is formed.

5 Divide the dough into four equal pieces. On a lightly floured surface, roll one piece of dough to a 12" x 5" rectangle. Spread one-quarter of the filling in a long, 2-inch strip along the center of the rectangle, leaving $1/2$-inch at each end. Fold up the dough, so the filling is covered completely, and pinch the ends together to seal. With a sharp knife dipped in flour, cut the roll into 16 slices. Place the slices, slightly apart on the prepared cookie sheet.

6 Bake the cookies 16 to 18 minutes, or until lightly browned. Transfer to a rack to cool. Continue making more cookies in the same manner until all the dough and filling have been used.

Yield: *64 cookies*

Italian Butterscotch Balls

This recipe is adapted from an old-fashioned Sicilian spice cookie that's primarily baked for Christmas. But these buttery butterscotch balls are so delicious, they're bound to become a year-round family favorite.
*Note: **You need to chill the dough at least 2 hours before baking the cookies.***

DOUGH

$^3/_4$ cup raisins

$1^1/_2$ sticks ($^3/_4$ cup) butter, softened

$^1/_2$ cup plus 2 tablespoons dark brown sugar

1 egg

$^1/_2$ cup butterscotch ice cream topping

$^1/_2$ teaspoon vanilla

$2^1/_2$ tablespoons water

$2^1/_4$ cups flour

2 teaspoons baking powder

$^1/_8$ teaspoon salt

$^3/_4$ cup finely chopped pecans

ICE CREAM TOPPING GLAZE

1 cup confectioners sugar

2 tablespoons butterscotch ice cream topping

4 teaspoons water

DOUGH

1 Place the raisins in a bowl, and pour enough boiling water over them to cover. Let sit 10 minutes. Drain the raisins and chop finely.

2 Meanwhile, in a large bowl, cream the butter with the brown sugar, beating until the sugar is fully incorporated. Beat in the egg, then the ice cream topping, vanilla, and water.

3 In another bowl, stir together the flour, baking powder, and salt. Add to the bowl with the creamed mixture and beat or stir until the dry ingredients are fully incorporated. Stir in the raisins and pecans.

4 Transfer the dough to a large piece of plastic wrap. Cover the dough, and chill at least 2 hours.

5 Preheat the oven to 350° F.

6 Grease one or more cookie sheets.

7 Break off a piece of dough and roll between the palms of your hand to form a ball about 1$\frac{1}{2}$ inches in diameter. (If the dough sticks to your hands, coat your palms lightly with flour.) Place the ball on the prepared cookie sheet. Continue making balls with the dough, placing them at least 1 inch apart on the cookie sheet.

8 Bake the cookies about 12 minutes. (The cookies will bake more evenly if you bake only one sheet at a time. If you prefer to bake 2 sheets at once, rotate them in the oven halfway through the baking period.) Transfer the cookies to a rack and let cool completely.

Ice Cream Topping Glaze

9 Stir together the confectioners sugar, ice cream topping, and water in a small bowl. Cover the tops of each cookie with a thin coating of glaze.

Yield: *About 40 cookies*

Knock-You-Nakeds

This is an old Southern recipe, traditionally made with chocolate ingredients. Once you taste these rich, gooey bars, you'll understand how they got their name, as they'll leave anyone awestruck. At any bake sale, these are the fastest items to go!

BOTTOM

1	package (about 18 ounces) yellow cake mix
$1/3$	cup ground hard butterscotch candy
$1/2$	cup chopped pecans
$1/3$	cup evaporated milk
$1 1/2$	sticks ($3/4$ cup) butter, melted

TOPPING

60	vanilla caramels (about 1 pound), unwrapped
$1/2$	cup evaporated milk
1	cup butterscotch morsels

1 Preheat the oven to 350° F.

2 Grease a 9" x 13" baking pan.

BOTTOM

3 In a large bowl, stir together the cake mix, butterscotch candy, and pecans. Add the evaporated milk and melted butter. Stir until well mixed. Spread in the prepared pan. Bake 20 minutes.

TOPPING

4 Place the caramels and evaporated milk in a medium saucepan. Cook over a very low heat, stirring frequently, until the caramels are melted and mixed into the milk.

5 Drizzle the caramel mixture evenly over the baked layer. Sprinkle with the butterscotch morsels. Return to the oven and bake 10 minutes longer. Transfer the pan to a rack to cool. Let cool completely before cutting into bars.

Yield: *30 bars*

Pecan Pie Squares

With a filling like classic pecan pie and a cookie-like crust, these squares are incredibly delicious. Ground butterscotch candy in the crust and butterscotch chips in the filling make this an even more delectable treat.

1 Preheat the oven to 350° F.

2 Grease a 9" x 13" baking pan.

EASY-MIX CRUST

3 In a bowl, stir together the flour, brown sugar, butterscotch candy, and salt. Add the butter and stir until crumbly.

4 With your fingertips, pat the mixture evenly into the bottom of the prepared pan. Bake the crust for 20 minutes.

FILLING

5 In a large bowl, beat the eggs well. Gradually beat in the brown sugar and corn syrup, continuing to beat until the mixture is thick. Beat in the butter and vanilla. Stir in the pecans and butterscotch morsels.

6 Spread the filling evenly over the crust. Return to the oven and bake 30 to 35 minutes longer.

7 Transfer the pan to a rack to cool. Cut into squares when completely cooled.

Yield: *24 squares*

EASY-MIX CRUST

2	cups flour
$1/4$	cup dark brown sugar
$1/4$	cup ground butterscotch candy
$1/8$	teaspoon salt
I	stick ($1/2$ cup) butter, melted

FILLING

3	eggs
I	cup dark brown sugar
I	cup dark corn syrup
2	tablespoons butter, melted
I	teaspoon vanilla
$1 1/2$	cups coarsely chopped pecans
$1/2$	cup butterscotch morsels

Double Butterscotch Bars

The dough for these bars is rich and chewy—like an oatmeal blondie. But what makes these exceptional for the butterscotch lover is the filling—dense and fudgelike, but with a wonderful butterscotch flavor instead of chocolate.

FILLING

1	11-ounce package butterscotch morsels
1	14-ounce can sweetened condensed milk
3	tablespoons butter
3/4	cup chopped pecans

DOUGH

2	sticks (1 cup) butter, softened
1	cup dark brown sugar
3	eggs
1	tablespoon vanilla
3	cups flour
2	cups rolled oats
3/4	cup ground butterscotch candy
2	teaspoons baking powder
1/4	teaspoon salt
1/2	cup chopped pecans

1 Preheat the oven to 350° F.

2 Grease a 9" x 13" baking pan.

FILLING

3 Place the butterscotch morsels, condensed milk, and butter in the top of a double boiler. Cook over boiling water, stirring often, until the butter and morsels are melted. Remove from the heat and stir in the pecans.

DOUGH

4 In a large bowl, cream the butter with the brown sugar, beating until the sugar is fully incorporated. Beat in the eggs, then the vanilla.

5 In another bowl, stir together the flour, oats, butterscotch candy, baking powder, and salt. Add the creamed mixture to the dry ingredients and beat until the dry ingredients are incorporated. The dough will be very stiff. Stir in the pecans.

6 Press a little more than half the dough evenly into the bottom of the prepared pan. (The easiest way to do this is to flour your hands lightly and press the dough with your fingertips.) Pour the filling over the dough. Drop the remaining dough by small spoonfuls evenly over the filling.

7 Bake the bars 35 minutes. Transfer to a rack to cool. Let cool completely before cutting into bars.

Yield: *36 bars*

Butterscotch S'Mores

Popular S'Mores ingredients—graham crackers, chocolate, and roasted marshmallows— are incorporated into these fabulous butterscotch bars. Serve them while still slightly warm from the oven for maximum resemblance to the S'Mores of your youth.

1 Preheat the oven to 350° F.

2 Grease a 9" x 13" baking pan.

BARS

3 In a large bowl, beat the eggs. Gradually beat in the brown sugar, continuing to beat until the mixture is thick. Beat in the melted butter, then the vanilla.

4 In another bowl, stir together the flour, baking powder, salt, crushed grahams, and ground butterscotch. Add to the egg mixture, beating or stirring until the dry ingredients are moistened. Stir in the pecans. Spread the batter evenly in the prepared pan. Bake the bars for 30 minutes.

TOPPING

5 Remove the pan from the oven. Sprinkle the bars evenly with the butterscotch and chocolate morsels, then the graham pieces, and finally the marshmallows. Return the pan to the oven and bake 12 to 15 minutes longer, or until the marshmallows are lightly browned. Transfer the pan to a rack to cool. Cut into bars when slightly cooled.

Yield: *30 bars*

BARS

4	eggs
1 1/2	cups dark brown sugar
1 1/2	sticks (3/4 cup) butter, melted
2	teaspoons vanilla
1 1/2	cups flour
2	teaspoons baking powder
1/8	teaspoon salt
4	whole graham crackers (5" x 2 1/2" each), crushed
1/2	cup ground butterscotch candy
1	cup chopped pecans

TOPPING

1/2	cup butterscotch morsels
1/2	cup semi-sweet or milk chocolate morsels
4	whole graham crackers, coarsely crumbled
2	cups mini marshmallows

Oatmeal Date Bars

These are the classic, immensely popular bars that feature a sweet, cookie-like crust, rich date filling, and crumbly oatmeal topping. While brown sugar and butter traditionally lend a subtle butterscotch flavor to the bars, I've enhanced this flavor through the addition of butterscotch candy and morsels.

FILLING

1	10-ounce container pitted dates, coarsely chopped (about 2 cups)
3/4	cup water
1/4	cup finely chopped butterscotch candy

DOUGH

1	stick (1/2 cup) butter, softened
1/2	cup dark brown sugar
1/4	teaspoon baking soda
1/4	teaspoon cinnamon
1/8	teaspoon salt
1 1/4	cups flour
1	cup rolled oats
1/4	cup chopped butterscotch morsels

FILLING

1 Place the dates and water in a small saucepan. Cook, stirring frequently, about 5 minutes, or until the dates are very soft and the water has been absorbed. Transfer the mixture to a bowl and let cool to room temperature while preparing the dough. When cool, stir in the butterscotch candy.

DOUGH

2 Grease a 9" x 9" square baking pan.

3 Preheat the oven to 350° F.

4 In a large bowl, cream the butter and brown sugar, continuing to mix until the sugar is fully incorporated. Beat in the baking soda, cinnamon, and salt. Add the flour and oats. Stir just until the mixture is crumbly.

Assembly & Baking

5 Measure out 2 cups of the oat mixture and place in the prepared pan. Using your fingertips, press into the pan to make an even layer of dough. Bake 10 minutes.

6 Stir the butterscotch morsels into the remaining oat mixture. Remove the pan from the oven. Carefully spread the date filling over the crust. Sprinkle evenly with the oat mixture.

7 Return the pan to the oven and bake 25 minutes, or until golden. Transfer the pan to a rack to cool. When completely cool, cut into bars.

Yield: *12 to 16*

Butter Toffee Bars

Here, a crispy butterscotch brownie-like crust is topped with melted butterscotch morsels and pecans to make a bar that is exceptionally appealing. The bars are a snap to make, which is a good thing, since they disappear about as quickly.

2	sticks (1 cup) butter, softened
2	cups brown sugar
1	egg
1	teaspoon vanilla
2	cups flour
$\frac{1}{3}$	cup ground butterscotch candy
1	11-ounce package butterscotch morsels
1	cup chopped pecans

1 Preheat the oven to 350° F.

2 Grease an 11" x 16" jelly roll pan.

3 In a large bowl, cream the butter with the brown sugar, continuing to beat until the sugar is fully incorporated. Beat in the egg well. Add the vanilla and beat again. Add the flour and beat just until it is incorporated. Stir in the butterscotch candy.

4 Spread the batter evenly in the prepared pan. Bake for 15 minutes.

5 Turn off the oven. Remove the pan from the oven and sprinkle the butterscotch morsels evenly over the top. Return to the oven for 2 minutes for the butterscotch to melt.

6 With a knife, spread the melted butterscotch morsels evenly over the bottom layer. Sprinkle with the pecans and press down lightly. Cut into bars while still warm. Transfer the pan to a rack to cool. When cool, remove the bars from the pan.

Yield: *35 bars*

Butterscotch Shortbread

Crisp, rich, light, and butterscotch flavored, this version of traditional shortbread can't be beat. What's more, it is incredibly fast and easy to make.

1 Preheat the oven to 325° F.

2 Grease a baking sheet.

3 In a large bowl, cream the butter with the brown sugar, continuing to beat until the sugar is fully incorporated. Add the cornstarch and flour, and beat until the dry ingredients are incorporated. Stir in the ground butterscotch morsels.

4 Divide the dough in half. With lightly floured hands, pat each half into a 7-inch circle on the baking sheet. Using a pizza cutter, divide each circle into 8 wedges, cutting through the dough completely.

5 Bake the shortbreads 25 minutes or until very lightly browned at the edges. Remove from the oven and immediately cut into wedges again with the pizza cutter. Let sit 5 minutes for the shortbreads to cool slightly. Then, with a spatula, carefully remove each wedge to a rack.

Yield: *16 shortbread wedges*

10 tablespoons butter, softened
$1/3$ cup dark brown sugar
$1/2$ cup cornstarch
1 cup plus 3 tablespoons flour
$1/2$ cup butterscotch morsels, finely ground

Carmelized Shortbread Bars

The crust of these bars—a thin butterscotch shortbread—is covered with a homemade caramel topping that literally melts in your mouth.

CRISPY SHORTBREAD CRUST

2	cups flour
$1/2$	cup brown sugar
$1/2$	cup ground butterscotch candy
$1/8$	teaspoon salt
$1 1/2$	sticks ($3/4$ cup) butter
$1/4$	cup water

TOPPING

$1 1/3$	cups dark brown sugar
$1/2$	cup heavy or whipping cream
$1/3$	cup dark corn syrup
3	tablespoons butter
1	teaspoon vinegar
$1/8$	teaspoon salt
1	teaspoon vanilla
$1/2$	cup butterscotch morsels
$1/2$	cup chopped pecans

1 Preheat the oven to 375° F.

2 Grease an 11″ x 16″ baking pan.

CRISPY SHORTBREAD CRUST

3 In a large bowl, stir together the flour, brown sugar, butterscotch candy, and salt until the sugar is incorporated and free of lumps. With a pastry cutter, two knives, or your fingertips, cut in the butter until the mixture resembles course meal. Add the water, and mix until the ingredients hold together.

4 With floured fingertips, press the dough into the prepared pan in an even layer.

5 Bake the crust about 15 minutes, or until lightly browned. Transfer to a rack to cool.

TOPPING

6 When the crust has completely cooled, combine the brown sugar, heavy cream, corn syrup, vinegar, and salt in a large saucepan. Bring to a boil, stirring often. Lower the heat so the mixture is barely boiling, and cook 5 minutes. Remove from the heat and stir in the vanilla.

7 Pour the mixture over the crust, spreading it evenly. Sprinkle with the butterscotch morsels and the pecans. Let sit until the topping has cooled. Then cut into bars.

Yield: *36 bars*

Cakes and Coffeecakes

Butterscotch Chip Cake

This is an easily-put-together, lightly flavored butterscotch cake that's enhanced with butterscotch chips and pecans.

I	stick ($^1/_2$ cup) butter, softened
I	cup dark brown sugar
$^1/_2$	cup granulated sugar
3	eggs
I $^1/_4$	cups milk
I $^1/_2$	teaspoons vanilla
2	cups flour
I	tablespoon baking powder
$^1/_4$	teaspoon salt
$^1/_2$	cup chopped butterscotch morsels
$^1/_2$	cup chopped pecans

1 Preheat the oven to 350° F.

2 Grease a 9″ x 9″ square baking pan.

3 In a large bowl, cream the butter and both sugars until the sugars are fully incorporated. Beat in the eggs, then the milk and vanilla.

4 In another bowl, stir together the flour, baking powder, and salt. Add to the creamed mixture, beating or stirring until the dry ingredients are incorporated. Stir in the butterscotch morsels and pecans.

5 Spread the batter evenly in the prepared pan.

6 Bake the cake about 40 minutes, or until a toothpick inserted in the center comes out clean. Transfer the pan to a rack to cool.

Yield: *12 servings*

Butterscotch Fudge Cake
with Fudgy Butterscotch Icing

A classic dense, fudge cake, but with a wonderful butterscotch flavor, rather than the usual chocolate. The icing is rich, thick and fudge-like, and intensely butterscotch.

1 Preheat the oven to 325° F.

2 Grease a 10-inch tube or Bundt pan.

CAKE

3 In a large bowl, cream the butter with the brown sugar, continuing to beat until the sugar is fully incorporated. Beat in the eggs very well. Beat in the milk and vanilla.

4 In another bowl, stir together the flour, butterscotch candy, baking powder, and salt. Add to the creamed mixture, beating or stirring until the dry ingredients are incorporated.

5 Spread the batter evenly in the prepared pan. Bake 1 hour, 20 minutes, or until a toothpick inserted in the highest part of the cake comes out clean. Transfer the pan to a rack to cool. Allow the cake to cool completely before frosting it.

FUDGY BUTTERSCOTCH ICING

6 Place the brown sugar, butter, evaporated milk, and salt in a medium saucepan. Bring to a boil. Boil, stirring continuously, for 3 minutes.

7 Remove the pan from the stove and add the baking powder and vanilla. Beat with an electric mixer 5 minutes, or until thickened. Immediately drizzle over the cake.

Yield: *16 to 20 servings*

CAKE

2	sticks (1 cup) butter, softened
2	cups dark brown sugar
5	eggs
1	cup milk
1	teaspoon vanilla
3	cups flour
$1/2$	cup crushed butterscotch candy
2	teaspoons baking powder
$1/4$	teaspoon salt

FUDGY BUTTERSCOTCH ICING

1	cup dark brown sugar
4	tablespoons butter
5	tablespoons evaporated milk
	pinch salt
$1/4$	teaspoon baking powder
$1/4$	teaspoon vanilla

Butterscotch Layer Cake

This cake has the texture of a perfectly made yellow layer cake, with the elusive fragrance of butterscotch. The icing is creamy, shiny and completely delectable.

CAKE

1½ sticks (¾ cup) butter, softened
1½ cups dark brown sugar
3   eggs
⅔ cup milk
1½ teaspoons vanilla
2½ cups flour
2½ teaspoons baking powder
⅛ teaspoon salt

SHINY BUTTERSCOTCH ICING

½   stick (¼ cup) butter
½   cup dark brown sugar
⅛ teaspoon salt
⅓ cup evaporated milk
2   cups confectioners sugar
½   teaspoon vanilla
3   tablespoons crushed
     butterscotch candy

CAKE

1 Preheat the oven to 350° F.

2 Grease and flour two 9-inch round layer cake pans.

3 In a large bowl, cream the butter with the brown sugar, continuing to beat until the sugar is fully incorporated. Beat in the eggs, then the milk and vanilla.

4 In another bowl, stir together the flour, baking powder, and salt. Add to the creamed mixture, beating or stirring until the dry ingredients are incorporated.

5 Divide the batter evenly between the prepared pans. Bake the cake 25 minutes, or until a toothpick inserted in the center comes out clean. Transfer the pans to a rack to cool. When completely cooled, remove the layers from the pans and ice.

SHINY BUTTERSCOTCH ICING

6 Place the butter, brown sugar, salt, and evaporated milk in a large saucepan. Cook, stirring, until smooth. Remove from the heat and beat in the confectioners sugar and vanilla.

7 Place one cake layer right side up on a serving plate. Transfer about ¾ cup of the icing to a small bowl and stir in the crushed butterscotch candy. Spread this over the top of the cake layer.

8 Place the second cake layer, also right side up, on top of the first. Spread the remaining icing on the top and sides of the cake.

Yield: 12 to 14 servings

Marbled Butterscotch Cake

The moistest pound cake ever! Furthermore, the cake is lovely to look at, with vanilla and dark butterscotch cake batters marbled together.

1 Preheat the oven to 350° F.

2 Grease a tube pan.

3 In a large bowl, cream the butter with the sugar, continuing to beat until the sugar is fully incorporated. Beat in the eggs, then the milk and vanilla.

4 In another bowl, stir together the flour, baking powder, and salt. Add to the creamed mixture, beating or stirring until the dry ingredients are incorporated.

5 Transfer half the batter to another bowl. Stir in the butterscotch syrup, butterscotch candy, and baking soda.

6 Drop several spoonfuls of the butterscotch batter into the prepared pan. Cover with several spoonfuls of the vanilla batter. Continue alternating the batters until all the batter has been used. With a knife, gently swirl the two batters together to create a marbled effect.

7 Bake the cake 1 hour, 15 minutes, or until a toothpick inserted in the highest part of the cake comes out clean. Transfer the pan to a rack to cool. Remove from the pan when completely cool.

Yield: *12 servings*

2	sticks (1 cup) butter, softened
2	cups sugar
3	eggs
1	cup milk
2	teaspoons vanilla
3	cups flour
2	teaspoons baking powder
$1/4$	teaspoon salt
$3/4$	cup butterscotch ice cream topping
$1/3$	cup ground butterscotch candy
$1/4$	teaspoon baking soda

Glazed Cupcakes

A shiny butterscotch glaze adds to the appeal of these unbelievably moist and fudgelike cupcakes. Because the cakes derive most of their flavor from butterscotch ice cream topping, buy the best brand you can find—preferably from an ice cream shop or one of the mail-order sources listed in this book.

CUPCAKES

6	tablespoons butter, softened
1	cup dark brown sugar
2	eggs
1	cup butterscotch ice cream topping
3	tablespoons milk
$1\frac{1}{2}$	cups flour
1	teaspoon baking powder
$\frac{1}{3}$	cup chopped butterscotch morsels

EASY BUTTERSCOTCH GLAZE

$\frac{1}{3}$	cup dark brown sugar
1	tablespoon milk
$1\frac{1}{2}$	teaspoons butter
$\frac{1}{8}$	teaspoon vanilla

CUPCAKES

1 Preheat the oven to 350° F.

2 Place cupcake liners in muffin tins. (The recipe makes 16 to 18 cupcakes, so if you don't have enough muffin cups for this amount, you will need to bake the cupcakes in batches.)

3 In a large bowl, cream the butter with the brown sugar, continuing to beat until the sugar is fully incorporated. Beat in the eggs. Then beat in the butterscotch topping and milk.

4 In another bowl, stir together the flour and baking powder. Add to the butterscotch mixture, beating or stirring until the dry ingredients are incorporated. Stir in the butterscotch morsels.

5 Fill the cupcake liners approximately $\frac{2}{3}$ full. Place the tins in the oven and bake 20 minutes, or until the cupcakes test done with a toothpick. Remove the cupcakes from the tins and let cool on a rack.

EASY BUTTERSCOTCH GLAZE

6 When the cupcakes are completely cooled, combine the brown sugar, milk, and butter in a small saucepan. Bring to a boil, stirring. Remove from the heat, and stir in the vanilla. Let the glaze cool about 10 minutes before using. Then spread in a thin layer over the top of each cupcake.

Yield: *16 to 18 cupcakes*

Double Butterscotch Cake

This is about as easy to make as a batch of brownies, yet a special delight for lovers of butterscotch. The batter is extra rich from the addition of cream cheese, and yummy butterscotch sauce fills little holes you make when the cake is done baking.

1 Preheat the oven to 325° F.

2 Grease a 9-inch square baking pan.

3 In a large bowl, cream the butter, cream cheese, and brown sugar, continuing to beat until the sugar is fully incorporated. Beat in the eggs, then the vanilla.

4 In a small bowl, stir together the flour, baking powder, and salt. Add to the creamed mixture, beating or stirring until the dry ingredients are incorporated. Stir in the butterscotch morsels.

5 Spread the batter evenly in the pan. Bake about 35 minutes, or until a toothpick inserted in the center comes out clean.

6 Immediately poke 25 holes, at 1-inch intervals, in the cake, using the handle of a wooden spoon. Using a teaspoon, fill the holes with the butterscotch ice cream topping.

7 Transfer the cake to a rack and let it cool before cutting.

Yield: 10 servings

2	sticks (1 cup) butter, softened
1	3-ounce package cream cheese, softened
1 1/4	cups dark brown sugar
3	eggs
2	teaspoons vanilla
3/4	cup flour
2	teaspoons baking powder
1/8	teaspoon salt
1/2	cup butterscotch morsels
5	tablespoons high quality butterscotch ice cream topping

Butterscotch-Graham Cake

This dessert combines a fudgy-textured cake with two layers of delectable graham crumb filling for a sensational treat for butterscotch lovers.
Note: Because the crumb mixture on the bottom of the cake can fall off easily, you need to serve this cake directly from the pan.

CRUMB MIXTURE

$1/4$ cup ($1/2$ stick) butter

$1/2$ cup dark brown sugar

$1 1/2$ cups coarse graham cracker crumbs

$1/2$ cup finely chopped pecans

$1/4$ cup crushed butterscotch candy

CAKE

$3/4$ cup ($1 1/2$ sticks) butter, softened

$3/4$ cup dark brown sugar

3 eggs

1 teaspoon vanilla

$1 1/2$ cups butterscotch ice cream topping

$1 1/2$ cups flour

$1 1/2$ teaspoons baking powder

$1/3$ cup chopped pecans

CRUMB MIXTURE

1 In a medium saucepan, melt the butter. Remove from the heat and stir in the brown sugar until the mixture is smooth. Add the graham cracker crumbs, pecans, and butterscotch candy, and mix well. Set aside while preparing the cake batter.

CAKE

2 Preheat the oven to 350° F.

3 Grease and flour a 9" x 9" square baking pan.

4 In a large bowl, cream the butter with the brown sugar, continuing to beat until the sugar is fully incorporated. Beat in the eggs thoroughly. Beat in the vanilla and butterscotch topping.

5 In another bowl, stir together the flour and baking powder. Add to the creamed mixture, beating or stirring until the dry ingredients are incorporated. Stir in the pecans.

6 Sprinkle half the crumb mixture evenly in the bottom of the prepared pan. Spread half the batter evenly over the crumbs. Repeat these two layers.

7 Bake the cake about 1 hour, or until a toothpick inserted in the center comes out clean. Transfer the pan to a rack to cool.

Yield: *14 to 16 servings*

Blueberry Crumb Cake

Cream cheese gives this coffeecake a wonderful fresh creamy flavor that goes particularly well with the plump blueberries scattered throughout the batter. The cake is layered with a fragrant butterscotch crumb mixture that browns deliciously when baked. Serve the cake warm or at room temperature.

Note: When buying oatmeal cookies for the crumb mixture, choose cookies that are somewhat crisp. Very soft, chewy cookies will become soggy when made into crumbs.

CRUMB MIXTURE

1 In a medium bowl, stir together the crushed cookies, brown sugar, and butterscotch candy. Add the butter and stir until well mixed. Set aside.

CAKE

2 Preheat the oven to 350° F.

3 Grease a 9" x 9" baking pan.

4 In a large bowl, beat the cream cheese with the brown sugar until the sugar is fully incorporated. Beat in the eggs well, and then add the vanilla.

5 In another bowl, stir together the flour and baking powder. Add to the cream cheese mixture, beating or stirring just until the dry ingredients are incorporated. Stir in the blueberries and butterscotch morsels.

6 Spread half the cake batter evenly in the prepared pan. Sprinkle with half the crumb mixture. Repeat these layers with the remaining cake butter and crumb mixture.

7 Bake the cake 40 to 45 minutes, or until a toothpick inserted in the center comes out clean. Transfer the pan to a rack to cool.

Yield: *12 servings*

CRUMB MIXTURE

2	cups crushed oatmeal cookies
1/4	cup dark brown sugar
1/4	cup ground butterscotch candy
6	tablespoons butter, melted

CAKE

1	8-ounce package cream cheese, softened
1	cup dark brown sugar
2	eggs
1	teaspoon vanilla
1 1/2	cups flour
2	teaspoons baking powder
1	pint blueberries, washed and picked over
1/2	cup butterscotch morsels

Butterscotch-Pecan Torte

A torte is a cake in which ground nuts, breadcrumbs, or, in this case, butterscotch morsels substitute for most, or all, of the usual flour. Beaten egg whites add volume and a wonderful texture that contrasts with the more substantial ingredients. This torte is made even more delectable by the addition of a butterscotch glaze.

*Note: **You cannot tip the finished cake out of the pan, so it's best to use a pan with removable sides, or a two-piece tube pan in which the sides are separate from the central tube and bottom.***

CAKE

7	eggs, separated
1	cup dark brown sugar, divided usage
1/3	cup (5 1/3 tablespoons) butter, melted
1	teaspoon vanilla
2	cups ground pecans
1	cup butterscotch morsels, finely ground
1/2	cup flour
1	teaspoon baking powder
1/4	teaspoon salt

GLAZE

1/4	cup dark brown sugar
1	tablespoon flour
2	tablespoons butter
2 1/2	tablespoons heavy or whipping cream
1/4	cup ground butterscotch candy

1 Grease and flour a tube pan.

2 Preheat the oven to 350° F.

CAKE

3 Prepare the cake batter: In a large bowl, beat the egg whites until stiff. Add 1/4 cup brown sugar, and continue beating until the sugar is fully incorporated. Set the bowl aside.

4 In another bowl, beat the egg yolks with the remaining 3/4 cup brown sugar until the mixture is thick. Beat in the melted butter and vanilla.

5 In a third bowl, stir together the pecans, butterscotch morsels, flour, baking powder, and salt. Add to the bowl with the egg yolks and beat until the dry ingredients are fully incorporated.

6 Stir about one-third of the egg whites into the bowl with the butterscotch. This will lighten the batter so it's less stiff. Now fold in the remaining egg whites, stirring gently until the batter is uniform.

7 Pour the batter into the prepared pan. Bake the cake about 55 minutes, or until a toothpick inserted in the deepest part of the cake comes out clean.

GLAZE

8 In a small saucepan, combine the brown sugar, flour, butter, and heavy cream. Cook over a medium heat, stirring frequently, until the butter has melted. Continue to cook, stirring constantly, until the mixture comes to a full boil. Remove from the heat, let cool slightly, and add the butterscotch candy.

9 When the cake is done baking, preheat the broiler. Spread the glaze evenly over the cake and broil, about 6 inches from the heat, about 1 minute, or until the glaze is bubbly. Transfer the pan to a rack to cool.

Yield: *10 to 12 servings*

71

Butterscotch Roll

Rolled cakes look and taste spectacular. This is a lovely, light butterscotch sponge cake that's filled with a devastatingly rich pecan custard. Rolled cakes may seem complicated to prepare, but they really are quite simple as long as you follow the directions correctly.

CAKE

CAKE

4	eggs
3/4	cup dark brown sugar
1	teaspoon vanilla
2/3	cup flour
1/4	cup crushed butterscotch candy
1/2	teaspoon baking powder
1/8	teaspoon salt
3	tablespoons confectioners sugar

PECAN CUSTARD FILLING

1	cup whole milk
3/4	cup dark brown sugar
3	tablespoons flour
2	tablespoons butter
1/8	teaspoon salt
3	egg yolks
1/4	teaspoon vanilla
1/3	cup ground pecans

1 Line an 11″ x 16″ jelly roll pan with waxed paper. Spray the paper with cooking spray.

2 Preheat the oven to 400° F.

3 In a large bowl, beat the eggs very well. Gradually beat in the brown sugar, continuing to beat until the mixture is very thick. Beat in the vanilla.

4 In another bowl, stir together the flour, butterscotch candy, baking powder, and salt. Add to the egg mixture, beating or stirring until the dry ingredients are incorporated.

5 Spread the batter evenly in the prepared pan. Bake the cake about 13 minutes, or until a toothpick inserted in the center comes out clean.

6 While the cake is baking, spread a clean dishtowel on the kitchen counter, and sprinkle it with confectioners sugar. As soon as the cake comes out of the oven, tip it upside down onto the dishtowel. Peel off the waxed paper, and roll up the cake, beginning with a short edge, jellyroll style, in the towel. Let sit until ready to fill.

Pecan Custard Filling

7 Place the milk, brown sugar, flour, butter, and salt in the top part of a double boiler. Place the pot directly on the heat and cook, stirring with a wire whisk, until bubbles form at the edge.

8 Meanwhile, in a small bowl, beat the egg yolks well. Gradually stir in about a half-cup of the hot milk mixture. Now place the pot over the bottom part of the double boiler, filled with boiling water. Add the egg yolk mixture and cook, stirring, until the mixture is slightly thickened. It will be like a thin custard sauce.

9 Remove the pan from the heat and stir in the vanilla and pecans. Transfer the custard to a bowl. Place plastic wrap directly on the custard to prevent a "skin" from forming. Chill until cold and firm.

10 When ready to fill the cake, unroll the cake and dishtowel. Spread the cake with the filling, and roll up (without the dishtowel). Transfer to a serving plate and chill until ready to serve.

Yield: 8 to 10 servings

Cream Cheese Butterscotch

Thimble Cakes

These two-bite, mini cupcakes are irresistible. The cake batter is richly butterscotch, and it's topped before baking with a luscious cheesecake mixture. The cakes are perfect for any type of buffet.

CHEESECAKE TOPPING

1	8-ounce package cream cheese, softened
1	egg
$1/3$	cup dark brown sugar
$1/8$	teaspoon salt
$1/2$	cup butterscotch morsels, finely ground

CAKE

2	eggs
1	cup dark brown sugar
$1/3$	cup ($5\,1/3$ tablespoons) butter, melted
$1/3$	cup water
1	teaspoon vanilla
$1\,1/2$	cups flour
$1/3$	cup crushed butterscotch candy
1	teaspoon baking powder
$1/8$	teaspoon salt

CHEESECAKE TOPPING

1 In a medium bowl, beat together the cream cheese, egg, brown sugar, and salt, continuing to beat until the mixture is smooth. Stir in the butterscotch morsels. Set aside.

CAKE

2 Place mini cupcake liners in 2 mini cupcake tins, each with 12 cups. (The recipe makes 40 to 48 mini cupcakes, so you will need to bake them in batches.)

3 Preheat the oven to 350° F.

4 In a large bowl, beat the eggs with the brown sugar until the mixture is thick. Beat in the melted butter very well. Beat in the water and vanilla.

5   In another bowl, stir together the flour, butterscotch candy, baking powder, and salt. Add to the egg mixture, beating or stirring until the dry ingredients are incorporated.

6   If your mixing bowl does not have a lip for pouring, transfer the batter to another container (such as a glass measuring cup) with a lip. Fill the cupcake liners a little more than half full with batter. Drop about a teaspoon of the cheesecake topping over the batter, and press down lightly.

7   Bake the cupcakes 20 to 25 minutes, or until a toothpick inserted in the center comes out clean. Transfer the cakes to a rack to cool. Continue making cupcakes until all batter and topping have been used.

Yield: $3^1/_2$ *to 4 dozen mini cupcakes*

75

Banana Butterscotch Cake

There are some people who enjoy crumb cakes only for the crumbly topping; this is a cake for them. Two thick layers of crumbs—enhanced with pecans and butterscotch morsels—are layered with a rich, moist banana cake.

CAKE

- 1 1/2 sticks (3/4 cup) butter, softened
- 1 cup dark brown sugar
- 2 eggs
- 1 1/2 cups mashed ripe bananas (about 2 large bananas)
- 1/2 cup buttermilk (or place 1 1/2 teaspoons vinegar in a measuring cup and add milk to the 1/2-cup line)
- 1 teaspoon vanilla
- 2 cups flour
- 1/3 cup crushed butterscotch candy
- 2 teaspoons baking powder
- 1/2 teaspoon baking soda

OATMEAL CRUMB TOPPING

- 1/2 cup flour
- 1/2 cup rolled oats
- 2/3 cup dark brown sugar
- 1 teaspoon cinnamon
- 1 stick (1/2 cup) butter, cut into small pieces
- 1 cup chopped pecans
- 1 cup butterscotch morsels

1 Preheat the oven to 350° F.

2 Grease a 9" x 13" baking pan.

CAKE

3 In a large bowl, cream the butter with the brown sugar, continuing to beat until the sugar is fully incorporated. Beat in the eggs well. Beat in the mashed bananas, buttermilk, and vanilla.

4 In another bowl, stir together the flour, butterscotch candy, baking powder, and baking soda. Add to the creamed mixture, beating or stirring until the dry ingredients are incorporated. Set the batter aside while you prepare the topping.

OATMEAL CRUMB TOPPING

5 In a large bowl, stir together the flour, oats, brown sugar, and cinnamon. With a pastry cutter, two knives, or your fingertips, work in the butter until the mixture resembles coarse meal. Stir in the pecans and butterscotch morsels.

6 Spread half the cake batter evenly in the prepared pan. Sprinkle evenly with half the crumb mixture. Repeat the layers.

7 Bake the cake about 40 minutes, or until lightly browned and a toothpick inserted in the center comes out clean. Transfer the cake to a rack to cool.

Yield: *15 to 18 servings*

Open-Faced Pear Torte

This dessert is like a cross between a tart and a cake. The bottom is thin, yet cake-like, and deliciously flavored with lots of ground pecans and butterscotch. Glazed pears, poached in a brown sugar syrup, top the crust. The torte makes a lovely, not-too-heavy dessert for summer and fall. Try it topped with whipped cream or ice cream.
Note: *After glazing the torte, you will have some extra syrup left over. This is delicious reheated and served as a sauce over ice cream.*

CAKE

8	ounces pecans, ground finely (about 2 cups)
3/4	cup dark brown sugar
1/2	cup flour
1/2	cup crushed butterscotch candy
2	eggs, beaten
1/2	stick (4 tablespoons) butter, melted
2	teaspoons brandy

TOPPING

3	firm, ripe pears, peeled, cored, and sliced
1	cup dark brown sugar
2	cups water
1	pinch salt
1	tablespoon butter

1 Preheat the oven to 350° F.

2 Grease a 9-inch round baking pan.

CAKE

3 In a large bowl, stir together the pecans, brown sugar, flour, and butterscotch candy. Add the eggs, melted butter, and brandy. Beat well. The mixture will be thick and sticky.

4 Spread the mixture in an even layer in the prepared pan. The easiest way to do this is to flour your hands and then pat it into a layer using your fingertips.

5 Bake the cake about 18 minutes or until lightly browned at the edges and baked through in the center. Transfer the pan to a rack to cool. Let cool completely before covering with the topping.

TOPPING

6 In a medium saucepan, bring the brown sugar, water, and salt to a gentle boil. Add the pears and simmer until just tender. This will take about 5 minutes, depending on how thinly they are sliced and the ripeness of the fruit. Remove the pear slices with a slotted spoon and place in a colander to drain completely.

7 Add the butter to the poaching liquid. Bring to a boil, and cook
   until the mixture becomes syrupy, about 20 minutes. Remove
   from the heat and let cool slightly.

8 Arrange the pear slices attractively over the cake. Drizzle with
   $1/4$ cup of the syrup. Serve the torte at room temperature.
   Refrigerate leftovers.

Yield: *9 to 12 servings*

Upside Down Cake

Butterscotch lovers may not have realized why they're so fond of upside down cakes. But the reason is simple: The pineapple (or other fruit) on top is surrounded by a gooey butterscotch glaze that also seeps into the cake. This version uses canned apricots, but you can substitute any favorite fruit.

TOPPING

- $1/2$ stick ($1/4$ cup) butter
- 1 cup dark brown sugar
- 1 cup chopped pecans
- 1 16-ounce can apricot halves, drained

CAKE

- 1 stick ($1/2$ cup) butter, softened
- $2/3$ cup dark brown sugar
- 2 eggs
- 1 teaspoon vanilla
- $1/2$ cup milk
- $1 1/2$ cups flour
- $1/2$ cup crushed butterscotch candy
- $1 1/2$ teaspoons baking powder
- $1/8$ teaspoon salt

TOPPING

1 In a 9- or 10-inch ovenproof skillet, melt the butter. Remove the pan from the heat and stir in the brown sugar. Sprinkle the pecans evenly over the bottom of the pan. Arrange the apricots attractively over the nuts.

CAKE

2 Preheat the oven to 325° F.

3 In a large bowl, cream the butter with the brown sugar, continuing to beat until the sugar is fully incorporated. Beat in the vanilla and milk.

4 In another bowl, stir together the flour, butterscotch candy, baking powder, and salt. Add to the creamed mixture, beating or stirring until the dry ingredients are incorporated.

5 Turn the batter into the prepared pan and spread evenly. Bake the cake 45 minutes, or until a toothpick inserted in the center comes out clean. Turn the oven off, and tip the cake out onto an ovenproof platter. Scrape off any topping that has stuck to the pan and put it back on the cake. Let the cake sit in the hot oven for 5 minutes to set the topping. Transfer the plate to a rack to cool.

Yield: *10 to 12 servings*

Cranberry Roll-Ups

This tart-sweet coffeecake consists of a rich biscuit dough that's rolled up with a fragrant cranberry-butterscotch filling and then cut into slices. The resulting roll-ups are baked atop a gooey brown sugar and butter base, which then becomes an icing.

FILLING

1 In a small bowl, toss together the cranberries, brown sugar, and butterscotch candy. Set aside.

PAN

2 Pour the melted butter in a 9-inch square pan. Swirl to coat the sides. Sprinkle the brown sugar over the butter.

DOUGH

3 Preheat the oven to 400° F.

4 In a large bowl, stir together the flour, brown sugar, and baking powder. With a pastry cutter, two knives, or your fingertips, cut in the butter until the mixture resembles coarse meal. Stir together the beaten egg and the milk. Add to the dry ingredients, and stir until mixed.

5 Turn the dough out onto a lightly floured board, and knead a few times until smooth and no longer sticky.

6 On a lightly floured surface, roll the dough into a 9" x 13" rectangle. Sprinkle with the filling mixture. Beginning with a long edge, roll up the dough, jellyroll fashion. Cut the roll into slices 1-inch thick. Place the slices on their sides, just touching each other, in the prepared pan.

7 Bake the cake about 25 minutes, or until a toothpick inserted in the dough comes out clean. Immediately tip the coffeecake out, upside down, onto a plate. Serve warm or at room temperature.

Yield: *9 servings*

FILLING
1 1/2 cups dried cranberries
2/3 cup dark brown sugar
1/3 cup crushed butterscotch candy

PAN
3 tablespoons butter, melted
2/3 cup dark brown sugar

DOUGH
2 cups flour
2 tablespoons dark brown sugar
1 tablespoon baking powder
1/3 cup (5 1/3 tablespoons) butter
1 egg, beaten
1/2 cup milk

Pecan Coffeecake

This ultra-rich coffeecake is positively irresistible to anyone who loves butterscotch. The cake has a streusel crumb topping and is drizzled with a brown sugar glaze, which makes it as appealing to the eye as to the palate.

CAKE

- 1½ sticks (¾ cup) butter, softened
- 1½ cups brown sugar
- 1 egg
- 1 tablespoon vinegar mixed with enough milk to make 1 cup liquid
- 1 teaspoon vanilla
- 2½ cups flour
- ⅓ cup finely crushed butterscotch candy
- 1 teaspoon baking soda
- ¼ teaspoon salt
- ½ cup chopped pecans
- ½ cup butterscotch morsels

BROWN SUGAR ICING

- ½ cup dark brown sugar
- 2 tablespoons milk
- 1 teaspoon butter

1 Preheat the oven to 350° F.

2 Grease a 9″ x 13″ baking pan.

CAKE

3 In a large bowl, using a pastry cutter, two knives or your fingertips, cut together the butter and brown sugar until the mixture is crumbly. Measure ¾ cup of this mixture and set aside for the crumb topping.

4 Add the egg to the bowl with the rest of the butter and brown sugar mixture, and beat until very smooth. Beat in the vinegar-milk mixture and vanilla.

5 In another bowl, stir together the flour, butterscotch candy, baking soda, and salt. Add to the first bowl, beating or stirring until the dry ingredients are incorporated.

6 Spread the mixture evenly in the prepared pan.

7 Add the pecans and butterscotch morsels to the reserved butter-brown sugar mixture and stir until crumbly. Sprinkle over the cake batter.

8 Bake the cake 35 to 40 minutes, or until a toothpick inserted in the center comes out clean. Transfer the pan to a rack to cool.

Brown Sugar Icing

9 When the cake is completely cool, place the brown sugar, milk, and butter in a small saucepan. Bring to a boil, stirring. Remove from the heat and let cool slightly. Drizzle over the cake.

Yield: *15 servings*

Oatmeal-Streusel Muffins

Unlike ordinary muffins, these are so delectably rich and sweet, you can eat them for dessert, so I've included them in the cake chapter. The muffins have a wonderful chewy texture from the oats, and a crunchy butterscotch streusel is inside and on top.

BATTER

1	cup rolled oats
$3/4$	cup flour
$3/4$	cup whole wheat flour
2	teaspoons baking powder
$1/4$	teaspoon salt
2	eggs, beaten
$3/4$	cup dark brown sugar
$3/4$	cup milk
$1/2$	stick (4 tablespoons) butter, melted

BUTTERSCOTCH STREUSEL

$1/3$	cup chopped pecans
3	tablespoons flour
3	tablespoons dark brown sugar
$1 1/2$	tablespoons butter
$1/3$	cup finely chopped butterscotch morsels

1 Preheat the oven to 375° F.

2 Grease 2 muffin pans. (You will be making 9 muffins.)

BATTER

3 In a large bowl, stir together the oats, flour, whole wheat flour, baking powder, and salt.

4 In another bowl, stir together the eggs, brown sugar, milk, and butter. Add to the bowl with the flour, and stir only until the dry ingredients are moistened.

5 Fill each of 9 muffin tins nearly halfway with the batter.

BUTTERSCOTCH STREUSEL

6 With a pastry cutter, two knives, or your fingertips, stir together the ingredients for the streusel.

7 Sprinkle 1 tablespoon of the streusel mixture in each tin. Fill to the top with the remaining batter. Divide the remaining streusel mixture over the tops of each muffin. Fill about one-third of each empty tin with water to prevent it from burning.

8 Bake the muffins 25 minutes or until a toothpick inserted in the center comes out clean. Transfer the pans to a rack to cool.

Yield: *9 muffins*

Coffeecake with Pears

This is a wonderful recipe for a special brunch. The butterscotch-flavored cake is rich with sour cream and moist with fresh pear chunks. A luscious butterscotch-pecan streusel forms a crunchy crumb topping. Warm and fragrant from the oven, this cake can't be beat!

BUTTERSCOTCH CHIP STREUSEL

$2/3$ cup dark brown sugar

$1/2$ cup flour

1 teaspoon cinnamon

4 tablespoons butter

$1/2$ cup chopped pecans

$1/3$ cup chopped butterscotch morsels

CAKE

6 tablespoons butter, softened

$1 1/4$ cups dark brown sugar

2 eggs

$1 1/2$ teaspoons vanilla

1 cup (8-ounce carton) sour cream

$2 1/2$ cups flour

$1/2$ cup crushed butterscotch candy

$1 1/2$ teaspoons baking powder

$1/2$ teaspoon baking soda

$1/8$ teaspoon salt

4 firm but ripe pears, peeled, cored, and cut into $1/2$" cubes

BUTTERSCOTCH CHIP STREUSEL

1 In a medium bowl, stir together the brown sugar, flour, and cinnamon. With a pastry cutter, two knives, or your fingertips, work in the butter until the mixture resembles coarse meal. Stir in the pecans and butterscotch morsels. Set aside.

CAKE

2 Preheat the oven to 350° F.

3 Grease a 9″ x 13″ baking pan.

4 In a large bowl, cream the butter with the brown sugar, continuing to beat until the sugar is fully incorporated. Beat in the eggs well. Beat in the vanilla and sour cream.

5 In another bowl, stir together the flour, butterscotch candy, baking powder, baking soda, and salt. Add to the creamed mixture, beating or stirring until the dry ingredients are incorporated. Fold in the pears.

6 Spread the batter evenly in the prepared pan. Sprinkle the top evenly with the streusel mixture.

7 Bake the cake 50 to 55 minutes, or until a toothpick inserted in the center comes out clean. Transfer the pan to a rack to cool. Serve the cake warm or at room temperature. Refrigerate any leftovers.

Yield: *16 to 20 servings*

Butterscotch Candies

and Other Delectable Treats

Old-Fashioned Butterscotch

If you love butterscotch candy, you should try making your own, as it's much better and more fresh-tasting than store bought. Candy-making is remarkably simple. The only special equipment you need is a candy thermometer, which can be found in most supermarkets.
Brown sugar is granulated sugar that's been processed with molasses. So the extra molasses in this recipe intensifies the flavor and adds a rich, dark color.

2   cups dark brown sugar
1   stick ($\frac{1}{2}$ cup) butter
2   tablespoons molasses
2   tablespoons water
2   tablespoons vinegar

1 Place all ingredients in a large, heavy saucepan. Bring to a boil over a fairly high heat, stirring until the sugar is dissolved and the butter has melted.

2 Place a candy thermometer in the saucepan, and keep the mixture at a gentle, rolling boil until the temperature reaches 298° F. Do not stir and do not cook over too high a heat or the mixture may burn.

3 While the candy is cooking, place a large piece of aluminum foil on your counter and lightly coat with cooking spray.

4 When the mixture has reached the correct temperature, remove the pan from the heat. Let cool slightly, so it is less runny. Then, using a teaspoon, drop spoonfuls of the candy on the foil, where it will flatten into discs.

5 As soon as the candy is cool enough to handle (and before it hardens!), roll each piece in the palms of your hand to form a round ball.

6 When the candy has cooled completely, wrap each piece in a small square of waxed paper. Store in a tin in a cool, dry spot.

Yield: *1 pound candy*

Mock Pralines

As deliciously addictive as real New Orleans pralines, but so easy to prepare, you can let your child make a batch.

1 Preheat the oven to 325° F.

2 Lightly grease an 11″ x 16″ jelly roll pan. Break each graham cracker into quarters and line the bottom of the pan, so the crackers are touching.

3 In a small saucepan, melt the brown sugar and butter, stirring. Bring to a full boil. Immediately remove from the heat and stir in the cream of tartar, then the pecans and butterscotch morsels. Pour over the graham crackers and, using a knife, spread evenly.

4 Bake for 10 minutes.

5 While still warm, separate the graham pieces and transfer to waxed paper to cool.

Yield: *48 pieces*

12	large graham cracker rectangles
1	cup dark brown sugar
10	tablespoons butter
$1/4$	teaspoon cream of tartar
$1/2$	cup chopped pecans
$1/2$	cup butterscotch morsels

Butter Nut Brittle

Made with either almonds or pecans, this is likely to be the most delicious nut brittle you've ever sampled. It's great when munched just plain and just as fabulous when crushed and sprinkled over vanilla, butterscotch or coffee ice cream. this brittle is also a key ingredient in butter Brittle Bread PUdding (page 28). For the Pudding, use pecans, rather than almonds, for a more pronounced butterscotch flavor.

$\frac{1}{2}$	cup water
I	dark brown sugar
$\frac{1}{2}$	light corn syrup
I	cup slivered almonds or pecan halves
$\frac{1}{4}$	teaspoon salt
I	tablespoon butter
$\frac{1}{8}$	teaspoon baking soda

1 Place the water in a heavy saucepan and bring to a boil. Remove from the heat, and add the brown sugar, stirring until dissolved. Return the pan to the heat and add the corn syrup, almonds or pecans, and salt. Cook, stirring occasionally, until the mixture reaches 290° F on a candy thermometer.

2 Remove the pan from the heat. Add the butter and baking soda, and stir until the butter has melted.

3 Coat a baking sheet with cooking spray. Pour the brittle mixture onto the sheet. Using two spoons, spread the mixture until it is in a single thin layer. Transfer the sheet to a rack and let the brittle cool completely. When cool, break the brittle into chunks. Store in an airtight tin.

Yield: *About 1 pound nut brittle*

Butterscotch Fudge

Also known as penuche, this ultra-rich candy is creamy, smooth, and wonderfully fudgy.

2   cups dark brown sugar
$^1/_8$ teaspoon salt
$^2/_3$ cup milk
$^1/_2$ stick (4 tablespoons) butter
1   teaspoon vanilla
1   cup chopped pecans, optional

1 Place the brown sugar, salt, and milk in a large heavy saucepan. Cook, stirring constantly, until the mixture comes to a boil. Lower the heat slightly and cover the pot. Cook for 3 minutes. (The steam will dissolve any sugar crystals clinging to the side of the pot and prevent them from making the fudge grainy.)

2 Remove the cover and cook the fudge at a slow boil, without stirring, until the mixture reaches the soft ball stage (238° F on a candy thermometer). If you don't have a candy thermometer, you can drop a droplet of the mixture into a glass of cold water. If the mixture has not cooked enough, it will just dissolve in the water. But when it reaches the soft ball stage, it will form a ball on the bottom of the glass.

3 Immediately remove the pan from the heat. Add the butter, but do not stir it into the mixture. Let the pan sit undisturbed until the mixture cools to about 110° F. The pan will feel slightly warm to the touch but not uncomfortably hot.

4 While the mixture is cooling, lightly coat a 9″ x 5″ loaf pan with cooking spray.

5 Beat the mixture with a heavy spoon until the butter is completely incorporated and the mixture becomes smooth. From this point on, you need to work quickly, as the fudge will begin to harden. Stir in the vanilla and pecans, if using, and then immediately spread the fudge evenly in the prepared pan.

6 Let the fudge sit until firm. Then tip out of the pan onto a cutting board. Using a sharp knife, cut the fudge into squares.

Yield: *About $^3/_4$ pound of fudge*

Easy Butterscotch Fudge

Fudge made with marshmallow fluff isn't the real thing, but it's so delicious and unbelievably simple to make, all butterscotch lovers should have this recipe in their repertoire.

1	1-pound box dark brown sugar (about 2 1/2 cups)
1	5-ounce can evaporated milk (about 2/3 cup)
$1/2$	stick (4 tablespoons) butter
$1 1/4$	cups marshmallow fluff
$1/4$	teaspoon salt
1	11-ounce package butterscotch morsels
$1/2$	teaspoon vanilla
$1/2$	cup pecans, optional

1 Grease a 9" x 9" pan.

2 Place the brown sugar, evaporated milk, butter, marshmallow fluff, and salt in a large, heavy saucepan. Heat over a fairly low heat, stirring, until the butter melts. Increase the heat to medium-high and cook, stirring, until the mixture comes to a full boil. Lower the heat so the mixture remains at a gentle boil, and boil, stirring, for 5 minutes.

3 Remove the pot from the heat and stir in the butterscotch morsels. Continue stirring until melted. Stir in the vanilla and the pecans, if using. Pour the fudge into the prepared pan and let cool. It will firm up as it cools. When cool, cut into squares.

Yield: *About 2 $1/2$ pounds*

Butterscotch Truffles

Mere words cannot convey just how incredibly rich and delicious these deeply flavored, immensely satisfying butterscotch candies are. What's more, unlike most candy, the truffles require no cooking, so they're a breeze to prepare. The candies keep well for 2 weeks at room temperature and practically indefinitely in the freezer.

Although the truffles call for a small amount of dried figs, even people who aren't crazy about this fruit should not be put off. The figs help hold the candies together but are virtually undetectable flavor-wise.

1 Place the figs, brandy, and water in a small saucepan. Bring to a boil. Lower the heat, and simmer the figs, covered, 10 minutes. Let cool slightly.

2 Place the pecan cookies in the bowl of the food processor. Process about 5 minutes or until the cookies turn almost into a paste. Transfer to a large bowl.

3 Add the brown sugar, pecans, flour, butterscotch morsels, and corn syrup to the bowl, and stir to mix well.

4 Place the figs and any liquid from the saucepan in the food processor, and process until puréed. Add to the bowl, and stir well.

5 Pour the granulated sugar onto a plate. Have ready a tin for storing the truffles.

6 Shape the truffle mixture into 1-inch balls. Roll each ball in the granulated sugar, shake off the excess, and place in the tin.

7 Cover the tin, and let the flavors mellow at least 1 day before serving.

Yield: *50 to 55 1-inch truffles*

4	ounces dried figs (about 6 large), stems removed
$1/2$	cup brandy
$1/4$	cup water
1	16-ounce package pecan shortbread cookies
1	cup brown sugar
1	cup finely chopped pecans
3	tablespoons flour
1	cup chopped butterscotch morsels
2	tablespoons dark corn syrup
$1/2$	cup granulated sugar

Candied Popcorn

Warning! This is the single most addictive snack food I've ever eaten. Do not plan to make it unless you have people to share it with or have exceptional willpower.

When most people think of Valentine's Day and other candy-giving occasions for lovers, their first thoughts are of chocolate. But you can be more creative—especially with the butterscotch lovers in your life—with a gift of a special butterscotch treat, such as this popcorn.

3	quarts (12 cups) popped corn (about $1/2$ cup unpopped)
1	cup pecan halves
1	stick ($1/2$ cup) butter
1	cup dark brown sugar
$1/4$	cup light corn syrup
$1/2$	teaspoon salt
$1/2$	teaspoon vanilla
$1/4$	teaspoon baking soda
1	cup butterscotch morsels

1 Preheat the oven to 225° F.

2 Toss the popped corn with the pecans and spread in a lightly greased large shallow roasting pan. Keep warm in the oven while preparing the glaze.

3 Place the butter, brown sugar, corn syrup, and salt in a medium-sized saucepan. Bring to a boil over a medium heat, stirring frequently. Boil for 5 minutes, stirring constantly. Remove from the heat and stir in the vanilla and baking soda.

4 Remove the popcorn mixture from the oven, and pour the brown sugar mixture over it. Working quickly, stir to coat the popcorn and nuts with the glaze. Spread out in the roasting pan.

5 Return to the oven and bake the popcorn 1 hour, removing it every 15 minutes to stir the mixture. After 45 minutes (the final time you remove the popcorn from the oven to stir it), add the butterscotch morsels, and continue baking for the final 15 minutes. Let the popcorn cool in the pan. When completely cooled, store in a covered tin.

Yield: *About 12 cups*

Rice Krispies Squares

Everybody's favorite, with a new twist. And, the recipe is so easy, even a child can make it.

3 cups crisp rice cereal, such as Rice Krispies

$3/4$ cup butterscotch chips

$1/3$ cup coarsely chopped butterscotch candy

2 tablespoons butter

3 cups miniature marshmallows

1 Coat a 9" x 9" square baking pan with cooking spray.

2 In a bowl, stir together the cereal, butterscotch chips, and butterscotch candy.

3 In a large saucepan, melt the butter over low heat. Add the marshmallows and cook, stirring constantly, until the marshmallows are melted. Remove from the heat and add the cereal mixture. Stir until the cereal is well coated.

4 Turn the candy into the prepared pan. Using a buttered plastic spatula or waxed paper, press the mixture down so it fills the pan evenly. Transfer to a rack to cool. When cool, cut into squares.

Yield: *20 squares*

Gourmet Butterscotch Goodies

A Mail-Order Treats Source Guide

Introduction to Sources

For those times when you're not in the mood to make it yourself, or when you want to indulge in a fabulous butterscotch treat (for yourself or for giving), I have compiled a selection of goodies available from companies around the country. Although these foods are found primarily in gourmet food shops, many of these companies have toll-free numbers and/or web sites that allow consumers to purchase directly from them by mail. A few of the companies ship only to specialty food stores. But if you call the company, they are happy to provide you with the name of the store closest to you. And, believe me, these delectable treats are well worth seeking out!

Candy

COUNTRY FRESH FUDGE

This Tennessee-based company makes more than 60 varieties of fudge, including two butterscotch flavors—Penuche and Penuche-Nut, both of which are available in 5-ounce gift boxes. "Penuche" is an odd word. According to *The Joy of Cooking*, penuche and butterscotch fudge are synonymous. But at most fudge shops, penuche refers to a maple-flavored confection. At Country Fresh Fudge, the flavor is only subtly butterscotch, not as pronounced as a butterscotch lover might prefer. But the texture and quality are superb.

SWEET CHARLOTTES

Charlottes, located in Northern California, makes an assortment of the best toffees imaginable. The flavor I'm recommending for readers of this book is Maple Butter Toffee. Although called "maple," the rich butter flavor predominates, so the candy is nearly butterscotch and definitely worth sampling. Each toffee is coated with a thick layer of milk chocolate.

MAGGIE LYON CHOCOLATIERS

Ever wonder, where candy stores that don't make their own candy, get their fabulous-looking truffles and other creations? One good possibility might be from this Georgia-based manufacturer of fine chocolates. Maggie Lyon makes about two dozen different varieties of truffles, including Butterscotch! This large, luscious truffle contains a rich butterscotch filling that's coated with milk chocolate and garnished with an attractive orange swirl. Order a box of butterscotch only, or mix with other flavors of your choice.

COUNTRY FRESH FUDGE
Phone: 1-800-545-8782
Fax: 1-423-435-1930

SWEET CHARLOTTES
Phone: 1-800-SWT-CHAR (798-2427)
Fax: 1-650-589-1923
Web Site: www.sweetcharlottes.com

MAGGIE LYON CHOCOLATIERS
Phone: 1-800-969-3500
Fax: 1-770-446-2191

Hagensborg Foods

Hagensborg, located in Washington state, imports a variety of foods, including several different kinds of candies. The line of "Meltaway Supremes" is made in Canada, and the Butterscotch French Silk Meltaways come individually wrapped in a little four-ounce carton. The candies have a texture that's a cross between caramel and fudge, with a wonderful butterscotch flavor and just a hint of chocolate.

Kopper's Chocolate Specialty Company

This company makes more than 250 varieties of chocolate-coated confections, including liquid-center cordials, coffee beans, dried fruits, and nuts. Fortunately, for lovers of butterscotch, there is one delectable candy made in this flavor—Milk Chocolate Butterscotch Balls—which have a chewy butterscotch center, surrounded by creamy milk chocolate.

Fran's Pecans

Like Kopper's, this North Carolina company makes an assortment of chocolate-coated nuts and dried fruits, although not in as many exotic flavors. Their Butterscotch Pecans are sensational—huge pecan halves, generously dipped in delectable butterscotch candy. The pecans come in a variety of attractive packages, including colorful tins, apothecary jars, boxes, and bags.

HAGENSBORG FOODS

Phone: 1-800-851-1771
Fax: 1-253-395-9365
Web Site: www.hagensborg.com

KOPPER'S CHOCOLATE SPECIALTY COMPANY

Kopper's does not sell directly to consumers. However, their candies are in wide distribution. Call or Fax for a retailer near you.

Phone: 1-800-325-0026
        212-243-0220
        (In New York City)
Fax: 212-243-3316

FRAN'S PECANS

Phone: 1-800-476-6887
Fax: 1-704-561-0078
Web Site: www.franspecans.com

EILENBERGER'S BAKERY AND NUTCRACKER SWEETS

This Texas company has been manufacturing cakes (such as triple chocolate fudge and old-fashioned pecan) for more than a century. They also sell nuts, and their Butterscotch Pecans taste very similar to those made by Fran's Pecans (page 102). I can't recommend one company over the other. Try them for yourself!

CAROUSEL CANDIES

Carousel specializes in a wide assortment of caramels, all tasting homemade. These are rich, melt-in-the-mouth candies of the sort you'll never find in the grocery store. The Butterscotch Caramels have a subtle, delicate flavor.

MY SISTER'S CARAMELS

This California company has been selling high-quality caramels for more than 20 years. The Butterscotch Cream caramels are rich, chewy, and not overly sweet and are available in cute corrugated boxes tied with colored rope or in embossed gold boxes. There's also a Caramel Apple Kit, which includes 12 ounces of Butterscotch Cream caramels, 4 sticks, and sprinkles for decorating the apples.

CLOUD NINE

Cloud Nine makes only natural confections that are sweetened with cane juice and contain no preservatives or additives. Ten percent of the company's products are donated to protect the Rainforest. Cloud Nine offers a wide range of treats, including immensely flavorful hard candy rolls, of which the Butterscotch flavor is definitely worth sampling (or even carrying in your pocket wherever you go).

EILENBERGER'S BAKERY AND NUTCRACKER SWEETS

Phone: 1-800-788-2996
Fax: 1-903-723-2915
Web Site: www.eilenberger.com

CAROUSEL CANDIES

Carousel does not sell directly to consumers. Call or Fax for a retailer near you.
Phone: 1-888-656-1552
Fax: 1-708-656-0010

MY SISTER'S CARAMELS

Phone: 1-800-735-2952
Fax: 1-909-798-7294

CLOUD NINE

Phone: 1-800-398-2380
Fax: 1-201-216-0383
Web Site: www.aarrgghh.com/
    cloudninecandy/
    products/htm

CLOVER LAND SWEETS

Phone: 1-800-277-3226
Fax: 1-334-227-4294

LAMMES CANDIES
SINCE 1885

Phone: 1-800-252-1885
Fax: 1-512-238-2007
Web Site: www.lammes.com

BEN & BILL'S
CHOCOLATE EMPORIUM

Phone: 508-696-0008
        (Martha's Vineyard, MA)
        508-548-7878
        (Falmouth, MA)
        413-584-5695
        (Northampton, MA)
        207-288-3281
        (Bar Harbor, ME)

CLOVER LAND SWEETS

This Alabama company makes a large variety of traditional candy-store items. But their truly unique item happens to be butterscotch flavored, and it is sensational. Called Southern Treasures, these contain a butterscotch-flavored cookie crust, which is covered with white chocolate, butterscotch morsels, and nuts. Each bar weighs 3 ounces and is irresistible. The company sells various sized gift boxes of the Southern Treasure bars.

LAMMES CANDIES SINCE 1885

This company based in Austin, Texas, makes just a few varieties of nut-based candies, the most delicious of which is their Texas Chewie Pecan Pralines. While most pralines are too sweet and not sufficiently butterscotch flavored, these are close to perfect—how a Southern grandmother would make them in her own kitchen.

BEN & BILL'S CHOCOLATE EMPORIUM

This store, with three locations in Massachusetts and one in Maine, makes the most sensational homemade ice creams and candies. One candy—Butternut Crunch—is especially popular (the store usually sells out the entire batch on the day it's made). The candy is a layer of butterscotch, dipped in chocolate, and coated with nuts. For maximum enjoyment, visit Ben & Bill's to sample goodies that can't be shipped (like their ice cream). But if this isn't possible, they do mail order their candies. Call any location for service.

Cookies and Baked Goodies

GOOD FORTUNES

For someone with a touch of whimsy, there's no better gift than cookies from this California company. And the gigantic fortune cookies (6 inches wide and nearly one pound in weight) make a perfect way to express your every thought, as Good Fortunes will insert the message of your choice inside. For butterscotch lovers, Good Fortunes makes three different products to choose from, all dipped in caramel toffee: Good Fortunes (a single gigantic cookie), A Dose of Good Fortunes (classic-sized fortune cookies), and Pretzel Wands.

WILLINGHAM MANOR

This is a family-owned company based in Atlanta that makes a variety of bite-size (about 1-inch across) cookies and savory crackers. For butterscotch fans, a good bet is the Pecan Sweete, which comes in 4-ounce boxes and 8-ounce tins. They are virtually impossible to distinguish from homemade butterscotch-pecan cookies.

POPPIE'S COOKIES

This company was started by a father who liked to bake cookies for the neighborhood kids and eventually began commercial preparation of his cookies, all made with the same ingredients as in his own kitchen. The Butterscotch with Pecans Cookies, for example, contain just sugar, flour, butter, eggs, pecans, salt, baking powder, and vanilla. The result tastes just like homemade. The cookies are tiny, thin, and crispy, and come packaged in an attractive silver box.

GOOD FORTUNES
Phone: 1-800-644-WISH (644-9474)
Fax: 1-818-595-1550
Web Site: www.the-wishlist.com

WILLINGHAM MANOR
Phone: 1-800-255-5323
Fax: 1-770-447-0406
Web site: box-of-goodies.com/wmanor.htm

POPPIE'S COOKIES
Phone: 1-800-666-4416
Fax: 1-312-640-0450
Web site: www.poppiescookies.com

105

Grand Avenue Chocolates, LLC

At present, this California-based company makes just a single product line—a delectable shortbread cookie. The Butterscotch Slumber variety (perhaps so-named because it will bring on daydreams of ecstasy) has a creamy butterscotch filling and is dipped in chocolate. It is positively irresistible.

Brent & Sam's Gourmet Cookies

Brent & Sam's makes crisp, buttery cookies packaged in cute, snack-size (2-ounce) and larger (7-ounce) bags, as well as attractive tins. This Little Rock company sells a Toffee Pecan cookie with a wonderful butterscotch taste.

Boulder Brownie Company

Named for the Colorado city where owner Richard Heller originally developed his recipe for these amazingly rich bar cookies, Boulder Brownies are actually made today in Stamford, Connecticut. Butterscotch lovers should try the Boulder Blondie: a classic blondie bar with chocolate chips and walnuts. Each 3-ounce bar comes individually wrapped.

GRAND AVENUE
CHOCOLATES, LLC

Unfortunately, this company distributes only to specialty stores. Call, Fax or check their Web site for a store near you.

Phone: 1-800-798-4322
Fax: 510-798-4387
Web site: www.grandavenue
chocolates.com

BRENT & SAM'S
GOURMET COOKIES

Phone: 1-800-825-1613
Fax: 1-501-568-9777
Web site: box-of-goodies.com/
brentsams.htm

BOULDER BROWNIE COMPANY

Phone: 1-800-309-9995
Fax: 1-203-323-2010
Web Site: www.boulderbrownie.com

Taste of Gourmet

This company originated as a restaurant, located in Indianola, Mississippi. The wonderful Southern pies prepared at this restaurant are so popular, the company decided to manufacture a mix so people everywhere can enjoy them. All you need to add is melted butter and eggs. The pie mixes come in cute little boxes, with or without a crust mix. (If you don't want their crust mix, you can make your own crust or buy a prepared crust from your supermarket's freezer case.) The company's butterscotch flavor pie is called Southern Praline (add your own pecans if you wish), and it has a wonderful brown sugar taste.

Breakfast at Brennan's

Anyone who's ever visited New Orleans is told to be certain to eat at Brennan's for a fabulously delicious breakfast. Now, some of the restaurant's specialties are available to everyone, whether they travel to New Orleans or not. One item not to be missed is their Pecan Praline Muffin Mix. Tender and flavorful, these are a snap to whip up any time you want a warm butterscotch flavored treat.

TASTE OF GOURMET
Phone: 1-800-833-7731
Fax: 1-601-887-5547
Web Site: www.tasteofgourmet.com

BREAKFAST AT BRENNAN'S
Phone: 1-800-888-9932
Fax: 1-504-283-2620

Snacks

KORNFECTIONS &
TREASURES TOO

Phone: 1-800-469-8886
Fax: 1-703-817-9560
Web site: hometown.aol.com/
        Krnfection/kornfl.htm

SAVANNAH CINNAMON
COMPANY

Phone: 1-800-288-0854
Fax: 1-912-233-3004
Web site: www.gardensgreen.com/
        GardenShed/savannah_
        mix_selections.htm

KORNFECTIONS & TREASURES TOO

If you like caramelized popcorn, you'll love the quality of this Virginia company's offerings. Fans of butterscotch will choose the Golden Butternut Korn, which contains 20% more butter than the other varieties and is loaded with almonds, cashews, and pecans. For those who don't care for nuts, Golden Butternut Krunch has the same coating, but without the nuts. Package sizes range from 4-ounce bags to 32-ounce pails.

SAVANNAH CINNAMON COMPANY

This company's original product was a cinnamon syrup, but they now make several other varieties, including Butterscotch. They also make another product from this syrup. Called Praline Crunch Savannah Squares, these combine a Chex-type cereal, syrup, and nuts and are every bit as delicious and irresistible as caramel popcorn. They're available in 4-ounce bags and 8-ounce boxes.

The Savannah Butterscotch Mix (syrup) comes with recipes. The manufacturer recommends adding it to iced coffee or ice tea in the summer and to warm milk in the winter (which makes a butterscotch version of cocoa). It can also be used as a topping for ice cream or oatmeal. The syrup can even be used to enhance your own butterscotch baked treats, such as butterscotch swirl brownies (add $1/2$ cup of syrup to an 8-ounce package of cream cheese and swirl with batter for blondies) or butterscotch poke cake (prepare any flavor cake in an oblong pan; while still warm from the oven, poke holes in the cake with a fork, and drizzle with butterscotch syrup).

Da Vinci Gourmet

If you've ever longed for butterscotch soda, just mix this company's Butterscotch Syrup with seltzer water (about one part syrup to six parts seltzer, or to taste) for a refreshing and unusual drink. The syrup is also delicious when added to coffee or as a light topping for ice cream.

Wabash Valley Farms

If you like the idea of making your own caramelized popcorn, this Indiana-based company makes a mix called Butterscotch Maple.

DA VINCI GOURMET
Phone: 1-800-640-6779
Fax: 1-206-764-3989
Web Site: www.davincigourmet.com

WABASH VALLEY FARMS
Phone: 1-219-253-6650
Fax: 1-219-253-8172

Sauces

WAGNER GOURMET FOODS

In 1847, John Wagner borrowed $2,000 to begin a specialty foods import business in Wilmington, North Carolina, geared toward upscale palates, such as the Waldorf-Astoria Hotel and the White House dining table of President Ulysses S. Grant. The original line of wines and exotic spices has been enhanced through the years to include a wide variety of foods, one of which is Butterscotch Sauce. It makes a perfect ice cream sundae.

TRADER VIC'S FOOD PRODUCTS

From the original Trader Vic's Restaurant established by Victor ("Trader Vic") Bergeron near San Francisco, this company has opened other restaurants throughout the world and also markets a variety of food products, including Pecan Praline Dessert Sauce, which is intended as a topping for ice cream or pound cake. This product is definitely for nut lovers, as the ratio of pecans to sauce is about fifty-fifty.

WAGNER GOURMET FOODS

Phone: 1-800-832-9017
Fax: 1-910-799-9745
Web Site: www.wagner-gourmet.com

TRADER VIC'S
FOOD PRODUCTS

Phone: 1-800-200-5355
Fax: 1-510-658-8110
Web Site: www.tradervics.com

PROVENDER INTERNATIONAL CORPORATION

Provender is an importer of sweet and savory foods and beverages, mostly from small European—primarily British—companies, two of which deserve special attention here. Mrs. Bridges manufactures a line of jams, preserves, and curds. Although "curd" is not well-known in the U.S., the texture is similar to lemon meringue pie filling and is wonderful when spread on biscuits or plain crackers and accompanied by a cup of tea. The Butterscotch Curd is a good bet for its intense flavor and smooth texture.

Even more unusual than butterscotch curd is the Butterscotch & Mascarpone Dessert Sauce made by English Provender. For those unfamiliar with mascarpone cheese, this is a soft, fresh cheese that's most often enjoyed here in the popular Italian dessert, Tiramisu. The Butterscotch & Mascarpone Dessert Sauce is sold in 7-ounce jars and can be used for dipping fresh fruit or spreading on slices of pound cake.

PROVENDER INTERNATIONAL CORPORATION

Phone: 1-800-678-5603
Fax: 1-201-662-1402

The King's Cupboard

Although not strictly butterscotch flavored, this company's Cream Caramel sauce is close enough and is certainly worth sampling, as it was a finalist at New York's Fancy Foods Show for "Outstanding New Product of 1996."

Steel's Gourmet Foods

Steel's is a family-run company in Bridgeport, Pennsylvania, that makes pie fillings, dessert sauces, jams, and syrups for flavored coffees. Although all their dessert sauces are excellent, the Butterscotch Sauce is particularly notable, as it's made with brown sugar butter and heavy cream. The sauce contains no additives, so it separates in the jar, just as a homemade sauce would. But a quick stir brings it back to a thick and gooey butterscotch sauce anyone would love over a scoop of ice cream.

THE KING'S CUPBOARD

Phone: 1-800-962-6555
Fax: 1-406-446-3070

STEEL'S GOURMET FOODS

Phone: 1-800-6-STEELS
Fax: 1-610-277-1228
Web Site: www.steelsgourmet.com

INDEX

(Italicized Items indicate Butterscotch Sources)

113

Did you find this book at the library?

Do you want your own copy, or do you want to purchase a copy for a friend?

ORDER ANOTHER COPY OF
THE BUTTERSCOTCH LOVER'S COOKBOOK

Send a check or money order for $17.95
plus $4.00 for postage and handling to:

Buttercup Press
321 Rutland Avenue
Teaneck, NJ 07666

Note: If ordering more than one copy,
postage is $2.00 for each additional book.